A World of
Differents

A World of Differents

Bob Laurent

Fleming H. Revell Company
Old Tappan, New Jersey

Library of Congress Cataloging in Publication Data

Laurent, Bob.
    A world of differents.

    1. Evangelistic work. I. Title.
BV3790.L253   248'.4   75-20290
ISBN 0-8007-0755-9

TO Dr. Benjamin P. Browne, the only man,
besides Jesus, who ever looked right through
me and saw that even I could help build
"A World of Differents"

Contents

Acknowledgments

Thank You, Lord, for my peculiar friends:

for Dave Nichols, and his gift for typing away my mistakes and golfing away my anxieties.

for Ralph Hunt, and his consistent friendship, encouragement, and pruning.

for my teammates on the Good News Circle, and their patience with my eccentricities and commitment to our common vision to reach the world with Jesus' love. Naturally, we may be a motley crew of musical misfits, but supernaturally, we've got a heavenly harmony going for us that just won't quit.

for my parents, and the inspiration I've drawn from their growing faith and firm resolution to be holy at all costs.

for Michael-Walters Industries and their lesson to me that Jesus is more than a match for the business world.

for Steve and Caryn, Bill, Mike, Linda, Jan, Bev, Kenny, Ray, Charlotte, Sonshine Circle, Joy, Jenny, Carrie, the Apostle Paul, President Ford, Henry Kissinger, Napoleon, Churchill, Lincoln, Houdini, O. J. Simpson, and all the rest of my close friends.

for Calvary Baptist Church in Schaumburg, Illinois, and its living proof that the Bible doesn't have to be the world's *least-read* best-seller.

But most of all, God, thanks for the three who wrote this book with me: my wife, Joyce, and my children, Christopher and Holly.

Preface

I have a heavy heart right now. I've been typing on this book for five days here at a family campground in southern Florida and I guess I'm getting lonesome for Christian friends. Christmas is just about three days away and I'm trying to finish it before the holidays are over.

The table where I'm working is only three feet off the main path that leads to the beach, and people keep looking at me out of the corner of their eyes as they walk past. I guess it isn't every day you see a guy in blue jeans with a four-day growth on his face, an electric typewriter and a picnic table. I've had plenty of chances to share with many people and tell them of my faith in Christ.

I'd rather be around the vacationing "camp set" with their hard-earned trailers and tents than the "jet set" with their luxurious vacation homes and private beaches. Campers are a friendly lot. It's kind of funny; a guy will see my Michigan license plates and excitedly approach me with, "Hi, I'm Don Dingledorf from Detroit. I see you're from Michigan, too."

I reply, "No, not exactly. I have friends in that state who loaned me their motor home, but actually I'm from Chicago."

"Oh," he says, not about to let this dampen his spirits, "Chicago's right next door to us. We're practically neighbors!"

I really appreciate his warmth and effort to find a common ground for friendship, but I can't keep from thinking he probably wouldn't even look up at me if we passed each other on the streets of Detroit. And now we're supposed to be long-lost brothers because we each have blue-and-white license plates?

In any case, he looks like he plans on staying for a while and he asks me the question I've already heard twenty-three times today from other genuinely interested campers: "What are ya' doin' there? Workin' on your master's thesis?"

"No, not exactly. I'm writing a book that I hope will be a contemporary look at what Jesus had to say about the life a Christian should live, and how we're supposed to be different from the rest of the world. That way the world will have a standard it can live up to instead of continuing down the tubes."

"Oh," he says, thinking to himself that I'm different all right, "That's nice. Uh-h-h, I'll see you later."

I've seen him a few times since, but he never stops long enough to talk.

It seems like I've tried just about everything to create a little healthy "Christian controversy" around this camp. I've been singing "The King Is Coming" every morning in the shower room and writing "Jesus loves you" in the sand. I even took a couple of hours out last night to construct a special Christmas banner on the back of our trailer that reads: HAPPY BIRTHDAY, JESUS!

But nobody seems to care. I'm beginning to think that if the Crucifixion took place here today, nobody would even turn out to see it.

My heart aches for these friendly folks. How wonderful it would be if they could find Jesus down here in the sunshine before they return north to their own bumper-to-bumper, tension-filled, frigid worlds.

You aren't feeling a little cold yourself, are you?

1
A Mountaintop Experience:
Take Your Pick

According to a recent survey the two most frequently asked questions in America are:

1. How can I get a parking place?
2. How can I lose weight?

I'm serious. This is no joke. Those are the two most overt concerns on the minds of most people around you. They are not unrelated, as I can see it might be a good deal easier for some of us to get a parking place if we'd lose a little excess baggage! But surely there are some heavier issues for us to attack.

Is there any way of getting Mr. Everyman, with his wallet full of promising credit cards and his premises full of menacing creditors, to wake up and stop following the crowd? He won't be any pushover, of that you can be sure, because he has had a lifetime of indoctrination in conformity.

Do you remember what it was like the first time you came home from school and said to your mother, "Mom, you've just got to let me go steady with Susy. We want to get married!"

And she wisely replied, "No, honey, I think eight years old is a bit young. Maybe in a couple of weeks. . . ."

And then you dropped the classic line that kids have been using since Adam and Eve raised a little "Cain" together: "But Mom, *everybody's doin' it!*"

The Great Clock-Watching Caper

That "everybody's doin' it" thing has gotten me into trouble more times than I like to admit. Once in junior high school, a couple of my friends came up to me and said, "Hey, Bob, we're going to pull a great trick on Mr. Evans. Will you help us?"

I wasn't the least bit interested. I knew Mr. Evans too well. He was so big that we called him "Goliath." In fact, rumor had it he was so big that when he lay around the house, he lay *around the house!*

I answered them right to the point. "No!"

That didn't stop them. They were too excited. "But, Bob, we've got a plan that's foolproof. We can't get caught."

I was interested.

I'd known for some time that Mr. Evans, my math teacher, had it in for me. I was one of the few students left in class that he hadn't found a reason to punish yet—mainly because I never did anything wrong, and I was the *sneakiest* spit-wad shooter in the whole school.

My diminutive desk sat in the shadow of his behemoth battleship, almost as if I were taunting him to raise his massive frame over his papers and squash me like a bug. But to my delight, it looked now like I would get him first—and without being punished!

Here was the plan. It was simple. It couldn't go wrong.

The final school bell rang every day at 3:15 P.M. When the clock hit 3:10 (this was one of those clocks where the minute hand waits sixty seconds and then jumps the full minute in one startling leap) all thirty-one of us were supposed to shove our books off our desks and then have five minutes to giggle about it, trying not to laugh right out loud at Mr. Evan's reddened, furious face. After all, what could he possibly do when every single student was in on it—even his favorite pets whom he wouldn't dare reprimand?

Yes, it truly was foolproof, and I was feeling pretty proud of myself for having the nerve to take part in this glorious scheme. But it actually wasn't that dangerous, was it? After all, everybody was doing it.

I watched the clock with all the intensity of a ravenous hawk eyeing its unsuspecting prey.

3:05   Just five more minutes. I wonder if Mr. Evans can hear my heart beat?

3:06   Oh, no! He's looking directly at me. He knows!

3:07   False alarm: he's calmly grading papers again, and doesn't seem to be aware that we're even in the room. It's going to work.

3:08   I sure hope he doesn't take a good look at this tremendous stack of books on my desk. I borrowed two extra history books just for the occasion.

3:09   Sixty seconds and counting. I wonder if this is how the astronauts feel?

That last minute seemed like an eternity. I counted it out as slowly as I could in my head, and still that minute hand didn't move. I sat on the edge of my chair, poised to strike quickly. I strained at the clock to see the first sign of movement, and finally eons later, the minute hand jumped the gap. With a hearty "Hi, Ho, Silver," and a lurching motion faster than a speeding bullet, I pushed all of the books off my desk. As I watched them crashing to the floor, I remember wondering if I had acted too soon.

It really didn't matter, because I soon realized I was the only one in class who had done anything! I had just handed Mr. Evans my head on a silver platter.

I looked up at him with a kind of sheepish grin and watched his lip curl up with a merciless this-is-too-good-to-be-true grin. I was wondering at that time if you could still go to heaven if you commit suicide, because I knew I just had!

Big Boys *Do* Cry

Do you see that this everybody's-doing-it attitude can be more of a headache than it's worth? It doesn't take much creativity or sensitivity to follow the crowd. Wouldn't it be refreshing some morning at high school to see a young guy open the front door for a disbelieving coed instead of rushing through it and slamming it in her face? Or offering her his place in the cafeteria line instead of cutting in front of her?

Now don't get me wrong. I don't mean to imply that chivalry is dead in our school systems today. I know there are plenty of guys who, when a girl drops her books in the hallway, will jump at the chance to kick them back to her.

The problem we have is that most young guys have been taught by their peers that when it comes to girls, they at all costs must be *cool;* they must maintain that fine edge of indifference and superiority even if their hearts are ready to explode with feeling.

This attitude carries over into the larger game of life, as evidenced by the male-female roles in a typical marriage. A lot of men make great campaign promises and then just don't follow up on them. For some it has been literally years since they have said a simple "I love you" to their wives or children. It's just not the way things are done. They have a masculine image to live up to, and that means there's not much room left for things like gentleness, vulnerability, and love.

Last summer I was sitting in the living room reading when I heard a terrible scream just outside my front door. Like most parents, I can distinguish my own children's crying, and so I flew out the door to the scene of the accident. There was my three-year-old son, Christopher, upside down and bawling, the victim of a hit-and-run collision with a Big Wheel.

In one fell swoop, I scooped him up and had both of us in the house and up in his bedroom before the neighbors suspected that my little man was a crybaby. I held him in my arms and said, "C'mon, son, let's dry those old tears up."

"But, Daddy, it hurts! Waaa-a-ah!"

Then I gave him my sternest look and exclaimed, "Look, son, *big boys don't cry!*"

As soon as that ancient bit of wisdom broke past my lips, I

got an immediate mental picture of a *Man* in His early thirties standing outside the tomb of His best friend, Lazarus, crying because it hurt so much. I saw a *Man* whose physical fiber had been hardened by years under the hot Galilean sun, now sitting on a hillside overlooking Jerusalem, crying because it hurt so much.

The One who went head to head with the money changers in the Temple;
  The One who ordered the roaring wind and the raging sea to be still;
    The One who now commands all authority in heaven and earth;

This same Man who never met a situation He couldn't handle, Could cry
  From the depths of a broken heart.

Yes, I guess big boys *do* cry.

Be Peculiar, Not Weird

The ability to give vent to your emotions and to have a sensitive attitude to those around you is only one area in which Jesus could make you different from the rest of the world. As John 8:36 AMPLIFIED says, "So if the Son liberates you—makes you free men —then you are really *and* unquestionably free." You are free to be out of step with the prevalent philosophy of "Do unto others before they do it to you," or "Do just enough to get by." You are free to stand alone sometimes against hatred and bigotry, against a world at war with itself, knowing that you and God together make a majority (Romans 8:31).

First Peter 2:9 KJV says that as a Christian you are a member of a "chosen generation, a royal priesthood, an holy nation, a peculiar people. . . ."

Titus 2:14 KJV states that Jesus "gave himself for us, that he might redeem us from all iniquity, and purify unto himself a peculiar people, zealous of good works."

So let's face it. If you want to follow Christ, you'd better be ready for a *peculiar* life-style. This doesn't mean you have to be an oddball fanatic or a spiritual recluse hiding out somewhere in a cave, but it does mean you will not be caught up in the universal descent to conformity, keeping up with the Joneses in their own efforts to keep up with declining world values. It does mean that you will be different. You will start "speaking truly, dealing truly, living truly—and so become more and more in every way like Christ . . ." (Ephesians 4:15).

Let's Make a Deal

Not long ago Madison Avenue lost one of its most desperate victims: *me!* I finally acted on something God's Word had convicted me about years earlier: I got rid of my television set. I traded it in on a Laymen's Parallel Bible and began trying to read this as much as I had been watching television. *It was one of the best deals I've ever made.* I started studying in Genesis, thinking it would take me years to read through the whole Bible, and three months after I buried the "tube," I finished the last chapter of Revelation. I also discovered I had a great deal more time to communicate with my wife and children. I found out their names and we became fast friends.

Those three months with the Bible are what really encouraged me to write this book. Every time I opened God's Word, I sensed the vast dichotomy between what the world had been trying to tell me to do with my life and the way that Jesus has so clearly shown.

Now tell me something: Would you be interested in finding out more about a way that promised genuine, lasting happiness and delivered it? A way that assures you of getting your material needs met and then shows you how? These truths and many more are found in the most famous of sermons, Jesus' Sermon on the Mount.

Sure, you're interested—if it works—but you're not so certain you want to be that "peculiar person" I've been talking about so far. Well, here are two good reasons for being different from the rest of the world.

1. *"For the Bible Tells Me So. . . ."*   God's Word is filled with strong calls for personal holiness. One of the major themes of the Old Testament is: "You shall be holy for I am holy" (*see* Leviticus 20:26). Then Jesus the Messiah, the very One whom the Old Testament had pointed to for hundreds of years, came on the scene and christened the body of His New Testament followers as the Church. What impresses me about this term that has become all too ordinary to us today is that its translation from the original Greek denotes qualities very *extra*ordinary. The word *church* actually means "that which is called out"—in other words, a separated community marching to the beat of a different drummer, an organization of believers that should be literally "out of this world."

The Apostle Paul says in Galatians 6:14, "As for me, God forbid that I should boast about anything except the cross of our Lord Jesus Christ. Because of that cross my interest in all the attractive things of the world was killed long ago, and the world's interest in me is also long dead." It sounds like Paul thinks he's found a big slice of freedom.

James, the brother of Jesus, very bluntly states, "Whosoever therefore will be a friend of the world is the enemy of God" (James 4:4 KJV). If the world has nothing to say against you, there's a good chance Jesus will have nothing to say for you when He pleads your case before the Father.

In heavy words Jesus Himself predicted how the world would receive those who carried the sign of the cross:

> If the world hates you, know that it has hated me before it hated you. If you were of the world, the world would love its own; but because you are not of the world, but I chose you out of the world, therefore the world hates you.
>
> John 15:18, 19 RSV

John, the son of Zebedee and the "apostle of love," sums things up pretty well by saying:

> Stop loving this evil world and all that it offers you, for when you love these things you show that you do not really love God; for all these worldly things, these evil desires—the craze for sex, the ambition to buy everything that appeals to you, and the pride that comes from wealth and importance—these are not from God. They are from this evil world itself.

> 1 John 2:15, 16

I realize that a person could run the wrong way with these Scriptures and interpret them to mean that a Christian should build an enormous glass dome around his life and keep a hands-off policy with the world. This is exactly the mistake of the Pharisees, whose hypocrisy Jesus so vigorously attacked, in their misunderstanding of God's Laws. For example, after just visiting the marketplace, they would come home and wash their bodies completely because of the spiritual contamination they felt from rubbing shoulders with the world. There was a holier-than-thou attitude in their worship, and I believe their sense of responsibility to others was just about zero. This is definitely not what the above Scriptures are all about.

2. *"What the World Needs Now. . . ."*   A Christian's life should be something very much akin to a clear beam of light leading the way out of darkness. When Jesus said, "You are the light of the world," I don't think He emphasized the word *light* any more than He did *world.* Light isn't really worth very much when it's hidden under a bushel basket, is it? A well-lighted house with no people in it is still empty. There's a power shortage in this world today in more ways than one, and I've met a few people who could certainly use a little light to brighten up their gloomy lives.

When Jesus taught, "Let what you say be simply 'Yes' or 'No' " (Matthew 5:37 RSV), I doubt very much that He was pushing just for less talk and more action. Instead, He could have been telling us that this world of situation ethics we live in, with its "do your own thing" and "everything is relative" approaches to existence, is in dire want of someone to come along and draw a few definite lines. We need absolutes. A positive *yes* and a positive *no*.

Several years ago I heard Dr. Francis Schaeffer of L'Abri Fellowship in Switzerland say, "If there is no absolute by which to judge society, then society itself becomes the absolute." There are several million Jews who will testify to this, and millions more who might still be alive if someone in Nazi Germany had realized the horrible truth of this statement and done something to correct it before it was too late.

Yes, life is important!

No, murder can never be justified!

It sounds a whole lot like "Thou shalt not kill," doesn't it?

Apathy: Who Cares?

I don't know about you, but I haven't heard much rumbling lately from psychologists advocating Dr. Spock's Corner. Could it be that a band of little Indians from his neighborhood has him tied up to a tree somewhere, and is now, with deadly rubber-tipped arrows, shooting holes in his nondisciplinary philosophies of raising children? Let's face it, without the Bible's absolutes— "He who spares his rod hates his son—But he who loves him disciplines him diligently" (Proverbs 13:24 NAS)—we have been raising a generation of disrespectful, disobedient little stinkers who are now having an awful lot of trouble getting along with anybody.

In the past decade or so, the children of our land have started questioning traditions at a feverish pace. They have succeeded in changing some things that needed it, and I suppose in a real sense their causes have approached the Cause that I propose—at least inasmuch as they have attempted to break out and be different. But this brings up a lesson that is so hard to learn: any effort to reach a fixed level of freedom without the One who said He was "the Way, the Truth, and the Life," must inevitably wind up far short of its goal. In fact, it will usually take its victim to a lower state of confusion and hopelessness.

For example, when the drug culture first started out with its patron saint, Timothy Leary, riding a crest of irrational but emotionally charged proclamations regarding the true peace, love, and freedom one could experience through a trip on LSD, it seemed to a lot of young seekers that the answer had come. There were all kinds of great "love-ins" with Woodstock as the granddaddy of them all.

But it wasn't long before the drug culture lost its innocence. At Altamont in California, the Rolling Stones hired the Hell's Angels to keep order at a rock festival and people started getting killed. It wasn't a game anymore. In Europe the same type of thing happened at the Isle of Wight Rock Festival. Approximately 480,000 people participated in what developed into one of the ugliest happenings ever. At the end of it, the fellow running the show grabbed the main microphone and just started screaming swear words at the crowd. The idea of a Utopian drug world began to seem more like a frightening pipe dream.

The mighty Beatles, of course, were the standard-bearers in the search for a final experience. From their early days as a "bubble gum" rock band, they moved into the drug scene and a new psychedelic sound. When these brought no lasting answer, their faces turned toward the East, and the guru led them on a precarious mystical path into nothingness. In their movie *Yellow Submarine*, they strongly indicate their belief that life is absurd and there is no hope left.

What scares me is that too many others are reaching that same conclusion today. Suicide is now the number two killer of teenagers in this country. And if suicide doesn't get them, apathy will.

A new bourgeoisie has formed around us and it has its own unique life-style. The only thing its members want is enough money to buy their "grass" and stay "up" as long as possible. They are convinced there are no real answers, so why bother to look? Why make any noise? Just enjoy what time you have under the sun, and when it's all over, that's it. There is no meaning to any of life.

I'm not naïve enough to believe I'm only talking about the far-out world of the adolescent. This problem of mistaken goals, misused talents, and misspent energies is universal. If you are not a Christian in every sense of that wonderful name, then you are very much affected, and you know it better than I.

To Walk Our Talk

We have a bona fide dilemma on our hands, and my question is—in view of our capacity to be the "light of the world," the call to be a "peculiar person," and the commission to act in the name of Jesus—*just what are we doing about it?*

By God's marvelous grace I am an integral part of the Body of Christ. To attack it would be like shooting off my own foot. Besides, I learned a long time ago that I don't *"go to church,"* I *am* the church. Because I love it and have given my life to further its work, I cannot help but sense there is something wrong within the ranks.

Now, before you start worrying about me, no, I don't believe God is dead. I don't even think He's the least bit sick. So the problem must lie with me and others like me. If you are alert to any degree at all, you must feel it, too. We've been trying harder than ever to get our churches going; these last twenty years have been full of amazing religious fervor, especially if money is any indication. But it seems we're spending more now and enjoying it less!

Despite all of our scurrying about, it certainly appears that we've lost unity and force as a movement in society. If there is any lesson for Christians to learn from Watergate or Vietnam, or from browsing the headlines in our daily papers, it's that our influence on this world of ours is less than ever. It would be disastrous for us to delude ourselves about this.

I believe our most fatal error has been our failure to exhibit to our children and to the watching world the fact that we really do take biblical truth seriously. One problem with posing as a Christian is that you can play the role for only just so long before someone catches you. I honestly don't know how we can expect our generation to take us at our word unless our words match up with our actions, until we are ready to practice what we preach —both the love of God and the holiness of God.

There must be content to our faith. Without consistent action, our faith smells of death (James 2:17). Unless we begin immediately to show the *love* of God to our neighbors, and the *holiness* of God in being able to say what's right is right and what's wrong is wrong, we will be forever shadowboxing in an arena that just doesn't exist.

Most people misinterpret Jesus' saying, ". . . you shall know the truth, and the truth shall make you free" (John 8:32 NAS). This verse should never be read apart from the one that precedes it, in which Jesus says to those who believed on Him, "If you abide in My word, *then* you are truly disciples of Mine." This means the prerequisite to constant freedom is knowing His Word and living it.

You know what beer made Milwaukee famous, what cigarette refreshes naturally, and what brand of panty hose will make you look eighty pounds thinner. These are the thoughts and ways of the world. Now God is inviting you to know His eternal love through His Son, Jesus. Quite a difference, isn't there? "For my thoughts are not your thoughts, neither are your ways my ways, saith the Lord" (Isaiah 55:8 KJV).

Being Different

Each night before I walk out on the stage to sing and preach, I bow in a "holy huddle" with my teammates on the Good News Circle. I can never be sure what person they'll come from, but I always know that I'll hear the same three prayers each time:

> Lord, don't let the crowd see us, but let them see You
> in us and give You all the glory.

> Lord, if You see the devil in this building tonight, tell
> him that we said he's a liar, and thank You for binding
> him in the strong name of Jesus.

and the prayer that best gets me prepared to go out on that
platform and share the Good News:

> Father, restore unto me tonight the joy of Your salva-
> tion. Thank You for saving my life, Lord.

What could possibly be more wonderful than to have your own
personal death sentence waived, and then have it replaced with
eternal joy? What a privilege it is to be a peculiar person, a citizen
of heaven, a king over life (see 1 Peter 2:9, Ephesians 2:19,
Romans 5:17).

Jesus said, "What is born of . . . the flesh is flesh . . . and what
is born of the Spirit is spirit" (John 3:6 AMPLIFIED). The former
is the world's way of giving birth (natural childbirth); the latter
is God's way (supernatural birth as a child of God). The former
lasts about threescore years and ten; the latter lasts forever.

Which way would you choose? It just doesn't make much sense
to follow the way of the world, does it? And yet, millions of people
are doing exactly that. A refreshingly candid Christian brother by
the name of Bob Benson illustrates the unreasonable, almost
ludicrous quality of choosing against God's salvation in his book
Come Share the Being. He likens the spiritually poverty-stricken
unbeliever who is offered grace by God to a hungry little boy on
a Sunday-school picnic who has nothing to eat but a dry baloney
sandwich in an ugly brown paper bag, and who finds himself being
offered a great chicken dinner by a generous Christian lady who
sets up her luscious banquet on a table right next to him. Of
course, the boy is going to trade his paper bag in on a succulent
drumstick. Benson relates:

> . . . and there you sat—eating like a king when you came
> like a pauper. . . . When I think about it like that, it
> really amuses me to see somebody running along
> through life hanging on to their dumb bag with that

stale baloney sandwich in it, saying, "God's not going
to get my sandwich! No sirree, this is mine!" Did you
ever see anybody like that—so needy—just about half-
starved to death, hanging on for dear life. It's not that
He needs your sandwich—the fact is, you need His
chicken.

What a privilege it is to share in this great banquet feast with
God's Son. It is really beyond me to think how much time pastors
and evangelists have to waste in getting people interested in
Christianity, when without all the promotional gimmicks and
clever buildups, the Gospel of Jesus Christ is the hottest, most
exciting piece of Good News that has ever exploded on this
planet.

Proverbs 16:20 RSV says, ". . . happy is he who trusts in the
Lord." That's probably why King David wrote: "I would rather
be a doorman of the Temple of my God than live in palaces of
wickedness" (Psalms 84:10). He was happier in his struggling to
be different from the rest of the world and have *life*, than selling
out to compromise and mediocrity.

As expected, there were times when David's friends thought he
was a little more than just "peculiar." One of my favorite stories
about David is found in 2 Samuel 6. As he is bringing the precious
Ark of the Lord into Jerusalem with great celebration, David is
so moved by the occasion that he starts leaping and dancing with
glee in front of the Ark and the city's entire population. I don't
think the Ark minded very much, but there was at least one
member of his public that was furious with him: his wife, Michal.
In fact, when she saw him carrying on she was "filled with con-
tempt for him." If my wife felt that way about me every time I
acted a little bit wacky, our marriage wouldn't have made it past
our three-and-a-half-day honeymoon.

Needless to say, David and Michal's wasn't doing very well
either. After her tongue-lashing, he curtly retorted, "I was dancing before the Lord . . . who appointed me as a leader of Israel.
. . . So I am willing to act like a fool in order to show my joy in

the Lord. Yes, and I am willing to look even more foolish than this . . ." (2 Samuel 6:21, 22).

The next verse gives us an idea about how serious David was in defending his sold-out and sometimes reckless-looking stand for Jehovah. It simply says, "So Michal was childless throughout her life." My wife and I have never gotten *that* mad at each other. Just ask our children.

Resurrection: You Can't Keep a Good Man Down

This wide-open, unpretentious attitude of David reminds me of a story about a young Christian guy sitting in the park on a warm summer's day, reading his Bible. He had just found out about Jesus' love a few days earlier, and now he couldn't get enough knowledge about this wonderful new world. He hadn't learned yet that it's simply not sophisticated to be enthusiastic about your faith.

The passage he was reading in Exodus that day was telling about the narrow escape of the Israelite children out of bondage in Egypt, and their miraculous crossing of the Red Sea when the waters parted and then re-formed to drown their Egyptian pursuers. (If you haven't read the Book, then maybe at least you've seen the movie. Remember Charlton Heston?)

It didn't seem to bother this young enthusiast that there was an unsuspecting park full of people who heard him exclaim when he couldn't restrain his excitement any longer, "Praise the Lord! Hallelujah! All those Egyptians! All that water!"

Caught unawares and enraged by this outbreak of unscholarly emotionalism, a misplaced theologian, who just happened to be walking through the park trying to figure out the number of angels he could get on the head of a pin, marched right over to our hero and firmly rebuked him: "You young whippersnapper! Don't you know that it wasn't 'all that water'? It's been proved there were only two inches of water!" Even though his statement wasn't true, the theologian stomped off in a huff, thinking there was one misguided fanatic who wouldn't be heard from again.

But just as he was getting out of earshot, he heard echoing through the trees, "Praise the Lord! Hallelujah! God drowned all those Egyptians *in just two inches* of water!"

Do you get the point? It's difficult to stop a genuine Christian, no matter what the odds are or where the opposition comes from. He believes in Matthew 17:20, which promises him nothing will be impossible to him, and Philippians 4:13 which says he can do all things through Christ Jesus, who supplies the strength. He knows you can't keep a good man down; that Jesus rose from that grave on the third day, and now is very much alive in himself and all other true Christians.

He wants to be different because God's Word says it's the only way, because the world is despairing for someone to come on the scene with a few absolute answers from which true guidelines for living can be drawn, and because this Holy Highway that God has mapped out for us leads to an abundant life that is possible to carry out in joy even when all around looks bleak, and an eternal life that begins the moment one receives Jesus as Saviour.

It's Not You Trying, It's Jesus Dying

Now we come to the real problem. You're probably saying, "This eternal, abundant, colossal, fulfilling, supercalifragilisticex-pialidocious life that God offers sounds great, but actually living it is another story. I've tried it, and it's just too hard."

Well, don't feel like the Lone Ranger, stranger. I've been caught spinning my religious wheels a few times, too, in my pathetic attempts to live the Christian life. Then I made the simple but well-hidden discovery that if it would ever be possible for me to go out and live it, then Jesus would never have had to face Calvary. Jesus is the only one who can live the Christian life, and He promises to do that by His Spirit within you. "Not by might, nor by power, but by my Spirit, says the Lord of Hosts" (Zechariah 4:6).

Jesus is still a carpenter, but now instead of working with His hands, He's working with our hearts; instead of building tables and chairs, He's in the business of building men and women into new creations. This is where the Sermon on the Mount comes in. I want you to consider it as *the* Carpenter's Blueprint for the Christian life.

Can't Anybody Get It Right?

A couple of weeks ago, I took my little boy to a junior high school football game. My next-door neighbor, who had just become a Christian at one of our rallies, was playing in the game. I wanted to go to encourage him in his young faith, and besides, I like football a lot. I've got to admit I didn't expect to see very much quality football, and I'll admit it—I didn't!

However, nobody can say it wasn't exciting or interesting. Yes sirree, sports fans, it amazed me how number 58, who couldn't have been more than 4'2" and 78 pounds, had the nerve to line up against a kid twice his size who consistently used the little fellow for a floor mat.

I've never seen so many comical broken plays, missed tackles, and touchdowns. I think the score was about 128 to 96 when darkness sounded its gun. That's the exciting part; now for the interesting.

The losing coach was a humorous study in frustration, although I don't think he saw much to laugh about during that long afternoon. When one of his players would catch a pass and start running toward the wrong goal, or when his quarterback would spot a man wide open and throw the ball on a pinpoint trajectory into the popcorn machine behind the bleachers, the coach's sideline antics and ravings would be hard to beat for sheer entertainment.

As the game wore on, it looked like he was going to have to pull out all the stops and spring his super secret-weapon play that would turn the momentum around in his favor, and send his team on to victory. I watched him grab a boy off the bench, intensely tell him the play, and then hustle him onto the field.

Then the curtain fell hard. That boy never even made it to the huddle. He got about three-fourths of the way there and fell flat on his face in the mud. I couldn't help but chuckle a bit.

I snapped out of it, though, when I heard the coach screaming across the field, pulling out the last of his hair and making Woody Hayes sound like a gentle conversationalist, "Can't anybody get it right!?!?"

As much as I've never appreciated pompous spewings from anybody's mouth, I must confess that many times I've found myself in that coach's cleats. Our team travels all over the country promoting the Christ of the Bible, His teachings and His love. But I just haven't seen enough people plugging in to it with any real depth of commitment or understanding. There are times when I honestly feel like crying out, "Can't somebody please get it right?!?!"

I'm not interested at this point in good intentions or half-baked attempts that wind up in compromise. The Apostle Paul never preached *tolerance;* he preached *conversion.* He was totally convinced that the Christian way was the right way and that anything else was a cheap substitute at best.

I'm not a mean man. I like children, family reunions, toothless dogs, and "The Waltons." It's just that I think too many of us are too easily pleased. The life Jesus constantly spoke of is not out of reach; it is possible.

On the front page of my Bible, I have carefully printed a slogan that came to me through my own powers of creative genius when I stole it off the front page of a friend's Bible. It says: "WHEN ALL ELSE FAILS, FOLLOW DIRECTIONS!"

The directions are right here in the Sermon on the Mount. He who has ears, let him hear.

2
Happiness Is Knowing Jesus

"Do you know what you're going to be when you grow up, Bobby?"

"Sure, that's easy. I'm going to be shortstop for the St. Louis Cardinals." I was ten years old and there was no doubt in my mind that my future was major league baseball. I was considering not even wasting my time playing Little League ball in Springfield, Illinois, but just moving on down to St. Louis where they needed me.

I started working out with an almost religious zeal. At the beginning of this intensive training, I was the weakest, skinniest bag of bones in my entire neighborhood, but I would go down to the basement almost every night and spend the evening with my no-money-back Charles Atlas course: push-ups, sit-ups, jumping jacks, and four-count burpies. Then after I worked up a good sweat with the calisthenics, I really got down to business with an exhausting weight-lifting program. I viciously attacked that weight-lifting bar, giving out with a loud yell (even before Kung Fu was popular), and with all the concerted thrust I could muster up, I powered that bar up, up, up, and jerked it cleanly over my head.

What a triumph! I set the bar down, *put the weights back on it,* and rolled it into the corner. I was going to be the biggest, strongest athlete around!

Unlike most guys who are turning into "Mr. Body Beautiful," I didn't check myself in the mirror every five minutes to see how it was going. In fact, I never looked in the mirror. I wanted to save it all up and see the amazing development in one admiring glance.

After months of these strenuous workouts, I decided it was time for the unveiling. I even rubbed baby oil all over my chest because I thought that's what Steve Reeves did to look so great in all those old Hercules movies. I boldly walked up to the full-length mirror, turned the light on, and took it all in very slowly. There I was—the new me: the greasiest, weakest, skinniest bag of bones in the entire neighborhood!

If anything, I looked even worse than before—kind of like a shiny clothesline pole, only I had more hang-ups. It was then I should have realized it was going to take a whole lot more than a major operation and a couple of bionic arms and legs to turn me into the Six-Million-Dollar Man. It looked like I had a great deal of time ahead of me as the $1.98 Runt!

But nothing was going to detour my efforts to be just like everybody else, to measure down to the world's expectations of me. After I finally gave up on the idea of catching the eye of a Cardinal scout, I graduated on to trying to impress teachers with good grades, parents with good manners, friends with good jokes, and girls with just about anything I could.

One day in high school during lunch hour I was standing around with a group of guys who were the rowdiest bunch of self-acclaimed swingers in the school. The only thing any of us knew about Jesus was that His last name was Christ. As we huddled in the hallway we started talking about either Einstein's theory of relativity or girls—I don't remember which. Suddenly, out of the girls' rest room (which coincidentally was right by the spot where we always stood) came the only girl in the whole school who could make the corneas of my eyes steam up when I saw her.

To my amazement—and my buddies' amusement—she walked right up to me and said very silkily, almost musically, "Hi, Bob." The guys seemed to notice right away that I wasn't ready for this bold greeting. Maybe it was the way the entire left side of my face started spasmodically twitching that gave me away. I don't know if that was it or not, but I do know I had terrible shooting pains in my eyebrows as I coughed out, "Uhh-h-h, Hi ya, Doris." I was such a witty conversationalist.

Fortunately everybody got in on the talking, so I could just stand there and watch her through the steam. As the bell rang and things began to break up, she moved toward me to say good-bye, and in doing so placed her hand on my right arm. Instinctively my arm went into a rigid flex, and she exclaimed in front of everybody, "Wow! You've really got a muscle there."

While I felt sure all of them could see my arm literally shaking off from its prolonged contraction, I quickly replied, "Yeh? You oughta feel it when I flex!"

Everyone was still watching; I hurriedly changed the subject and succeeded in pulling one of the worst moves of my teen years. Very few guys are honest enough to admit they've done something as corny as this, but most of us have. I tightened up my abdomen as solid as I could, and said through clenched teeth, "C'mon, Doris. Hit me in the stomach as hard as you want. It won't even hurt me."

This was too good to miss. Late for class or not, the crowd seemed to swell as it gathered around us. The main problem as I saw it was that Doris's biggest asset was not her beauty, but her athletic prowess: she was strong.

"Are you serious, Bob? I can hit you as hard as I want?"

"No problem," I cockily replied, but I was certain the great beads of perspiration on my forehead were betraying the quiver in my liver. I thought I caught a wild glimmer in her eye as she reared back, wound up, and buried her fist in my middle.

She pulled back waiting for me to fold. She wasn't the only one. The guys looked silly with their mouths open. I looked at her as straight as I could with crossed eyes and repeated myself: *"No problem!"*

Then I politely took my leave, walked around the corner, opened up my locker, and lost everything I'd just had for lunch. I thought I was going to die!

I don't believe I've ever really gained anything by trying to impress people; it's a game for losers, and the world can keep it.

Spiritual Myopia

Jesus has some good advice for us:

> "Do not lay up for yourselves treasures on earth, where
> moth and rust consume and where thieves break in and
> steal, but lay up for yourselves treasures in heaven,
> where neither moth nor rust consumes and where
> thieves do not break in and steal. For where your trea-
> sure is, there will your heart be also."
>
> Matthew 6:19—21 RSV

We are a people with a problem: we value things that fall apart.
It's hard to find a toy today that interests your kids that doesn't
cost at least ten or fifteen dollars. That's a lot of money for some
of us and it's been known to arouse ugly feelings within me when
I see Christopher banging away so hard on his brand-new Evel
Knievel Stunt-Cycle that the wheels fall off and the head rolls. I
just thank the Lord he usually plays with the boxes his toys come
in, for at least three good months.

Material things don't last. We fall for the world's come-on to
go for the quick buck, the fast deal, and the thrill of the moment.
Instead of giving our best to the Master, we give our best to
Master Charge. And eventually the fantasy world we've built by
living beyond our means and above our level of competency
comes crashing down on our spinning heads. The moth and rust
of a decaying society take their toll.

Where did we go wrong? From this vantage point it looks like
spiritual bankruptcy. *Things* seem more important to us than our
own souls. Jesus makes sense when He says, "What profit is there
if you gain the world—and lose eternal life? What can be com-
pared with the value of eternal life?" (Matthew 16:26).

David says: ". . . we are but dust, and . . . our days are few and
brief, like grass, like flowers, blown by the wind and gone forever"
(Psalms 103:14–16). God offers more. First Peter 1:4, 5 promises,
"And God has reserved for his children the priceless gift of eternal
life; it is kept in heaven for you, pure and undefiled, beyond the

reach of change and decay. And God, in his mighty power, will make sure that you get there safely to receive it, because you are trusting him."

We are suffering from what I call "myopia of the soul," which simply means spiritual nearsightedness. Our vision for anything other than our own mundane material needs is anemic. A man can look up at the sky on a starry night and notice only mysterious little silver dots. He has "ho-hum vision."

The alternative is to see into the depths of the constellations and be inspired enough to write, "When I consider Your heavens, the work of Your fingers, the moon and the stars, which You have created, what is man, that You are mindful of him?" (*see* Psalms 8:3, 4) That is "spiritual vision." This is why I appreciate so much the key thought in 2 Corinthians 4:18 RSV ". . . we look not to the things that are seen but to the things that are unseen; for the things that are seen are [brief and fleeting], but the things that are unseen are eternal."

Being stared at because of a plastic beauty created by a multi-million-dollar cosmetics industry;
Being praised and applauded for your successes over others;
Being able to procure more food than can be eaten,
More clothes than can be worn,
More rooms than can be lived in,
More wealth than can be spent.
If these and others like them make up your goals,
You are probably more nearsighted than you think.
You'd better enjoy them while they last,
Because they won't.

But a rich man should be glad that his riches mean nothing to the Lord,
for he will soon be gone,
like a flower that has lost its beauty
and fades away, withered—
killed by the scorching summer sun.

So it is with rich men.
    They will soon die and leave behind
        all their busy activities (James 1:10, 11).

We need something that exists beyond the hour, and beyond the grave. We need permanent values that really work. We need lasting happiness.

Enter the Beatitudes—the "beautiful attitudes"—of Matthew 5. Each "attitude" begins with the word *happy*, and before you write it off as high-sounding religious rhetoric, let me inform you that I know some real live human beings who have tried these and found them true. But here's fair warning that you may find them to have "the taste you hate twice a day." They don't sound too happy. You might react the same way that people did when Jesus said, "Love your enemies," instead of: "Hit 'em while they're down" to a world conditioned by a win-at-all-cost philosophy.

If the Beatitudes bother you that much you could be in serious trouble, because we are told: "The word of the cross *is foolishness* to those who are *perishing*" (*see* 1 Corinthians 1:18).

Even though I'm involved in a full-time, evangelistic ministry, I never get tired of preaching that what the Church needs is not better evangelistic campaigns to attract outsiders, but simply for its own people to begin to live the Christian life. I honestly believe that if every self-attested Christian did that for a full week, we would have a revival on our hands that would threaten to pack every pew in the country. That's why the Sermon on the Mount and especially this section on the Beatitudes is so important. It destroys our illusions about what great religious people we are. It shatters our false ideas and tells us in a hard-hitting yet positive way exactly how Jesus expects us to live the peculiar Christian life-style.

FROM RAGS TO RICHES

"Happy are the poor in spirit, for theirs is the kingdom of heaven" (*see* Matthew 5:3).

The first time I heard that phrase I was confused. Why should a person be happy or blessed if he was in poor spirits? But a little research brought out its true meaning. William Barclay says in his commentary, *The Gospel of Matthew* in the Daily Study Bible series: ". . . in Hebrew the word 'poor' was used to describe the humble and the helpless man who put his whole trust in God." So if you're trying to find a man in the Bible who was poor in spirit, don't look in the direction of Herod, Judas, Caiaphas, or Pilate—all men who were obviously undernourished spiritually. Instead—

Look into the spirit of a man like Gideon,
　Who, when the Lord turned to him and said,
　　"I will make you strong! Go and save Israel,"
　　　Sincerely replied,
　　　　"Sir, how can I save Israel? My family is the least in
　　　　the whole tribe, and I am the least in my family!"
　　　　(*See* Judges 6:15.)
　But God was looking for a man exactly like this,
　　And so He answered,
　　　"But I, Jehovah, will be with you" (v. 16).
Look into the spirit of a man like Moses,
　Who willfully threw his own life on the rocky altar of
　Mount Sinai,
　　Fasting and praying for forty days and nights
　　　To change God's mind about destroying the rebellious
　　　Israelites.
Look into the spirit of a man like David,
　Who though he was a mighty king
　　Cried out,
　　　"Save me, O God, because I have come to you for
　　　refuge. You are my Lord; I have no other help but
　　　yours" (Psalms 16:1, 2).
Look into the spirit of a man like Isaiah,
　Who though he was a great prophet
　　Could only say,
　　　"My doom is sealed, for I am a foul-mouthed sinner, a
　　　member of a sinful foul-mouthed race: and I have
　　　looked upon the King, the Lord of heaven's armies"
　　　(Isaiah 6:5).

Look into the spirit of a man like Peter,
> Who was the iron-willed member of Christ's select inner circle,
>> And yet exclaimed in the presence of Jesus,
>>> "Oh, Sir, please leave us—I'm too much of a sinner for you to have around" (Luke 5:8).

Look into the spirit of a man like Paul,
> Who was the great apostle,
>> But was forced to say after looking deep within,
>>> "Wretched man that I am! Who will deliver me from this body of death?" (Romans 7:24 RSV).

Look into the spirit of a man like John the Baptist,
> Who paved the way for Christ's ministry
>> By crying in the wilderness,
>>> "I baptize with water: but among you stands one whom you do not know, even he who comes after me, the thong of whose sandal I am not worthy to untie" (John 1:26, 27 RSV).

The important thing for you to notice here is that these men were not like this naturally. Almost all of them displayed egotistical, aggressive spirits. But here is the central glory of the Gospel: Jesus Christ can take the proudest of men and change them into men who are "poor in spirit." The Bible says God doesn't use many influential and powerful people, ". . . not many of high and noble birth" (1 Corinthians 1:26 AMPLIFIED). Instead, God has deliberately chosen: ". . . what in the world is foolish to put the wise to shame, and what the world calls weak to put the strong to shame" (v. 27).

This thought should give us great hope. It means we don't have to waste our time trying to impress God or other people. Maybe it's not so awful after all if I'm not an All-American football player, captain of the cheerleading squad (which wouldn't have gone over very big for me in high school anyway), president of the student body, a rising young executive, or one of a new breed in this country called "the achievers." Jesus has Good News for us:

we can be poor in spirit, and that means we can be different. We can depend on Him and He will make us new creations (2 Corinthians 5:17). And it doesn't matter who we are or what we think we can or cannot do.

When you get out of the way, God will be with you. You see, He doesn't recognize competition. If you are seeking for a name before men, there's a good chance yours will never make it into the Lamb's Book of Life (Revelation 20:15).

Remember that Jesus lavished three years of His attention on a highly fortunate group of twelve men who couldn't boast of their Ph.D.'s, scholastic aptitude, or worldly success. He didn't go down to the University of Southern Jerusalem and hold interviews. When He talked to a prospective disciple, He simply said, "Follow Me, and I will make you become fishers of men" (Mark 1:17 NAS).

He didn't say, "Follow Me—you're naturally an extroverted person, and I think you'd be pretty good at witnessing. I need your type on My staff!" No, He said, "I will make you *become*." In other words it still holds true that God will not recognize competition. He cannot use small-minded men and women living in mutual conceit. But God delights in taking "not many mighty, not many strong" and blessing them beyond their highest prayers.

A Winning Streak

Of course, this could mean that in your present position of heart and mind you're not very usable. You might need a little breaking before God can start making.

There is a beautiful illustration of this in the Gospel of Mark. In fact, the entire book serves as a confirmation that God can best use men and women who have plumbed the depths of personal failure, who know what it's like to be lower than the bottoms of their shoes. I say this because the beloved author of this book, perhaps the most graphic, forceful, and dramatic of all the Gospel accounts, can hardly claim a very prestigious beginning for his ministry.

It all started back on that crucial night in the Garden of Gethsemane when Jesus was arrested. It was a Friday, and young Mark—better known as J. M. by his friends—had spent the evening with his buddies cruisin' around Jerusalem on their camels. After getting home, he'd put on his pajamas and decided to curl up in front of an old rerun of "The Ten Commandments" before hitting the sack. Suddenly the network broke in with a terrible news report: there was an all-points bulletin out on the controversial young Nazarene, Jesus. The police were looking for him everywhere.

J. M. had a deep love and reverence for this disturbing teacher who called Himself the Son of God, and he was frightened to hear He was in danger. Without telling his mother where he was going —and without changing out of his pajamas—J. M. ran out of his house to go warn Him. He could have broken an Olympic record as he sped across the Kidron Valley and up into the Garden where he knew Jesus and the Twelve liked to meet.

He got there just as things started getting hot. A group of military police and religious leaders were storming through the Garden with their flashlights and guns, searching for their Victim. They didn't have much problem finding Him, since it seemed Jesus wasn't trying to escape.

J. M. was wondering how they found out His whereabouts when, to his disbelieving eyes, he watched one of Jesus' own staff members, Judas, step out of the enemy's ranks and kiss his Master. This served only to confuse the frightened lad, who looked pretty comical standing there in his pajamas with his eyes bugged out.

Then Jesus came forward and said, "Who are you looking for, men?"

They answered Him, "Jesus of Nazareth."

His eyes seemed to flash as He fearlessly replied, "I am He!"

They drew back and like a row of dominoes fell to the ground. If the circumstances had been different, it might have been hilarious. But it wasn't, and soon the ugly band was on top of Him with handcuffs and ropes.

Impetuous Simon Peter, one of the original "Bold Ones,"

caused quite a commotion by leaping out and taking on the whole bunch with just his Boy Scout knife. Either he had a lot of faith or he wasn't playing with a full deck, because Peter's dumb move created some tension among the troops and it looked for a while like Jesus wasn't going to be the only one busted.

The police were now giving the old evil eye to all of Jesus' comrades. J. M. got spooked and started to run, but before he could make any ground, a long hairy arm reached out and seized him. Though the grasp was firm, it didn't slow the lad down in the least: it just removed his pajamas, and he ran away naked!

I think J. M. probably took the long way home that night through the darkest back alleys of Jerusalem. Try to imagine his embarrassment as he sneaked around his house looking for an open window and finding none; he streaked for the front door only to find it locked!

Now put yourself in his poor mother's slippers. She answers the light tapping at the door with her bleary eyes and unsuspecting heart condition. "John Mark! Where have you been? I mean, what have you been doing? I mean, where are your clothes?!?!"

"Uh, Mom, can I answer those inside? It's kind of cold out here."

"You get in here right this minute and start talking."

"Aw, Mom. It was terrible. Not only did they get Jesus, but they got my clothes, too. Everybody saw me—*all* of me! I've never been so humiliated in my whole life. I'll never be able to face those guys again."

Chopping Down the Family Tree

It's lucky for all of us that John Mark never carried through with that emotional outburst. Just as Jesus broke the bonds of death, so Mark broke through all the barriers the world threw up at him to become the author of a book that has blessed millions and personally touched my own life right when I needed it.

Mark reminds us that even at our worst, we can become God's best. Who cares if you're not "God's gift to women," or the most beautiful girl on your block, or whatever else the world tries to make you think you've got to be in order to rate on somebody's meaningless chart? On a scale of one to ten, God's love for you goes right to the top.

A lot of people around me seem to be pushing for a cheap kind of immortality. They want to be remembered after they're gone so they leave instructions that their names be sculptured in granite. They spend senseless money on the genealogy racket, going hundreds of years back into their past just to dig up their relatives' moldy old heroics and sins. I refuse to waste my time on that bunk. If any of my relatives in the far distant future (if there is one) start constructing the Laurent family tree, when they come to my name they'll have to make a new branch for the majestic name of Jesus, because when I became a Christian, Romans 8:15 says I was adopted into a new family. Besides, I never wanted my name taken for "granite."

BLESSED ARE THE MEEK, NOT THE WEAK

"Happy are the meek, for they shall inherit the earth" (*see* Matthew 5:5).

When you think of someone who is meek, I don't want you to picture that mousey little next-door neighbor of yours who eats Lucky Charms for breakfast and wears white sox to church on Sunday, because that's my favorite cereal and I've got more white leggings than I know what to do with.

I would like you to meet the meekest man in the world. He said, "I am gentle and humble in heart," (*see* Matthew 11:29 NAS) and yet He was the same Man who stood His ground defiantly against the devil in the wilderness, the same One who drove the money changers out of the Temple. His name, of course, is Jesus.

Numbers 12:3 KJV tells us: "Now the man Moses was very meek, above all the men which were upon the face of the earth." Again we have no milk-toast, spineless character here. Moses was as tough as they come and could blaze out in righteous anger when the situation called for it.

It is clear then that our society's connotation for *meek* falls far short of its original meaning. Perhaps the closest English word to its true translation is *gentle*. With no apologies to the Archie Bunkers of the world, I think *gentle* is more fun to be around than *crabby*. What's wrong with just being nice once in a while?

Have you noticed how it seems to be in vogue these days to have a critical, cutting sense of humor? Some people can't seem to open their mouths without unloading some type of venomous comment. And even though most of it is done in fun, it doesn't seem to accomplish very much. Eventually someone always gets hurt, and seldom do the people involved really get to know each other.

There's much more than this to being meek. I believe that it's saying, "Happy is the man who has enough humility to admit his weaknesses and confess his needs." This is probably the most difficult of all the Beatitudes for me. I have always been a proud man, building walls around my faults, and hoping no one would break through to see the real me. I am fortunate that God cares enough to pierce those phony barriers and expose me for what I am, and help me become what He wants me to be.

I guess there's never been a time when I didn't want to be the leader in everything: choosing up sides for a sandlot baseball game; running for class office; even being the president of my own evangelistic ministry. Separate Jesus from me, and I'm a glory-hound. I always have been. It seems to be the nature of the beast to thrive on pride and self-esteem—but I'm probably more of a "beastie" than most.

The problem with this position is that the Bible says, "Pride goes before destruction, and haughtiness before a fall" (Proverbs 16:18). This certainly proved to be true in the devil's case when, because of his hunger for power, he took the long plunge from being Lucifer, the son of the morning, to Satan, the father of lies. He's been going downhill ever since, and as you can probably guess, I've had more than one fall myself.

I've learned a valuable lesson from this challenge in the Sermon on the Mount to be meek, as I've discovered why Jesus has been exalted to the right hand of the Father (Ephesians 1:20), and why He was made the "highest Ruler, with authority over every other power" (Colossians 2:10). The answer is found in Philippians, which says:

> Your attitude should be the kind that was shown us by Jesus Christ, who though he was God, did not demand and cling to his rights as God, but laid aside his mighty power and glory, taking the disguise of a slave and becoming like men. And he humbled himself even further, going so far as actually to die a criminal's death on a cross. Yet it was because of this that God raised him up to the heights of heaven. . . .

Philippians 2:5–9

Jesus broke through to Bethlehem and never stopped healing, washing feet, listening, and loving. I believe He really enjoyed this role of constantly giving, because He had His Father's leadership principles down so well. Instead of "first come, first served," He said He came to serve and not to be served. Then He told us to do the same. You see, He wants our Christian life to be as sound as possible so that we may lead others out of the darkness. He is giving us the key to unleashing all the strength available. It sounds like this:

> ". . . . Anyone wanting to be a leader among you
>   must be your servant.
>   And if you want to be right at the top,
>   you must serve like a slave" (Matthew 20:26, 27).

> "For anyone who keeps his life for himself
>   shall lose it;
>   and anyone who loses his life for me
>   shall find it again" (Matthew 16:25).

> ". . . for when I am weak,
>   then I am strong . . . (2 Corinthians 12:10).

In other words, the best way to become a leader is to learn how to follow; and Jesus said, "If anyone wants to be a follower of

mine, let him deny himself and take up his cross and follow me"
(Matthew 16:24).

Knowing our own limitations, letting Christ turn our weaknesses into strengths, and confessing our needs, we Christians can
become some of this world's all-too-rare "gentle people," sowing
love where hate has gone before.

An added bonus is that through your meekness you will inherit
the earth: "And since we are his children, we shall share his
treasures—for all God gives to his Son Jesus is now ours too"
(Romans 8:17). If our group ever needs a piece of land, I'm toying
with the idea of going into the real-estate office, looking the
realtor straight in the eye, and saying, "Do you just want to give
it to us right now, or should we wait and inherit it later?"

BLESSED ARE THE BROKENHEARTED

"Happy are they that mourn, for they shall be comforted" (*see*
Matthew 5:4).

The Arabs have a proverb that says, "All sunshine makes a
desert." I'm thankful for the infectious joy a smile can bring, but
I've always been somewhat suspicious of those Christians who
maintain a twenty-four-hour-a-day Pepsodent smile. You can just
picture them lying in bed at night struggling to keep the sparkle
going in their sleep.

Romans 12:15 says, "When others are happy, be happy with
them. If they are sad, share their sorrow." True spiritual mourning can show us better than anything else the genuine love of our
friends. Even better than that, it reveals the great heart of a
compassionate God. "Cast all your anxieties upon him, for he
cares about you" (1 Peter 5:7 RSV).

This brings out a truth that is diametrically opposed to the
thinking of a greedy world established on the grab-it-and-growl
syndrome. It is simply this: *Christianity is caring.*

This world's philosophy reads, "Forget your troubles; turn your
back on them. Do everything you can *not* to face up to them.
Escape into a fantasy world of sex, drugs, and alcohol."

Jesus is looking for someone, though, who *cares* about the problems around him. I've felt for a long time that the way of Christ is the most challenging because it hurts to taste the salt in someone else's tears; to meet reality head-on; to care intensely for the sufferings, sorrows, and needs of others.

There is also the *inward* look of mourning, and this is the hardest. It's easier to help other people get straightened out before we do our own "housecleaning." As Christians we usually have a defective doctrine of sin and joy. We need to cry out with Paul, "I know that nothing good dwells within me. . . . Oh, unhappy man that I am! Who will release me from my slavery to this deadly lower nature?" (*see* Romans 7:18, 24). That's the sin part; we need to face up to it, confess it.

But then Paul says, "Thank God! It has been done by Jesus Christ our Lord. He has set me free" (Romans 7:25). Admitting your sins to God doesn't just mean that He finds out about them, it means you get rid of them and find yourself free for the first time in your life. That's the joy part.

If there's going to be any mighty work of the Spirit of God in these last days, it will come through Christians who realize their old worldly life is through and they quit hankering for it, longing for it, and living it. They must agree with God that they are finished with it and it now nauseates them.

I don't know about you, but I've experienced enough joy from having Jesus around that I now *hate* the sin in my life. It is detestable to me because it slows me down and takes up valuable time that I could be using to love my family a little more.

First John 1:8, 9 was written to me as a believer:

> If we say that we have no sin, we are only fooling ourselves, and refusing to accept the truth. But if we confess our sins to him, he can be depended on to forgive us and to cleanse us from every wrong. . . .

I need to start consistently turning my back on sin, start mourning for it, and stop playing with it, fooling with it, exercising it, and rationalizing it. Only when that happens will there be a new release of the power of a resurrected Christ within my life.

According to Romans 6, when I became a Christian, I died with Christ when He died, and now I can share in His new life. It is stated that sin's power over me was broken and my old sinful nature was shattered. I know it sounds improbable, but I really don't have to sin anymore.

The standard cop-out that most Christians use—"Well, I'm only human. I'm bound to sin a little bit"—has no place in the theology of a New Testament believer. The Good News is that you're not "bound" to sin anymore. You've been released from its oppressive power over you by the death and Resurrection of Jesus. God says, "Reckon yourselves to be dead to sin and alive through Christ" (*see* Romans 6:11).

Life After "Birth"

"Happy are the pure in heart, for they shall see God" (*see* Matthew 5:8).

I did a lot of mourning in my early years of high school, but it was the kind that reeks with self-pity. I didn't like my complexion. I didn't like my weight (I was tired of having only one stripe on my pajamas). And I didn't like the way my hair stood up kind of funny in the back. In fact, I didn't like very much of me at all.

Of course, I heard all about how much more important it is to be beautiful on the inside than the outside, how God cares more about the picture than the frame. These may be very helpful thoughts for a homely *Christian*, but I still didn't know who Jesus was.

In my second year of college I finally faced up to the fact that my picture was even uglier than my frame. I could get a dermatologist to clear up the blemishes, drink milk shakes to put on weight, and pay a hair stylist to fix my cowlick, but who was going to correct my *inside* problem—the picture? Who could I find to answer questions like—

"Who am I?"

    "What am I here for?"

        "Where do I go from here?"

I've found only one Man who could ever help me with things like this. His name is Jesus: "And there is salvation in no one else, for there is no other name under heaven given among men by which we must be saved" (Acts 4:12 RSV).

That word *salvation* is the key one. Without it the picture will never improve. I had a "nature" problem, and I've always had it. David declares, ". . . I was born a sinner, yes, from the moment my mother conceived me" (Psalms 51:5). Until I read that verse, I used to think that babies and small children were the pure-in-heart ones. But now I'm the father of two darling little "rug rats" of my own and, much as I adore them, they have done a pretty good job of living up to the description given to all of us by Ephesians 2:3, that we are "by nature the children of wrath," like the rest of mankind.

The world seductively flatters us with, "You're not getting older, you're getting better." But the truth is obvious: we definitely are not getting any younger, and if you think we're getting better, then take another look around and guess again.

You've got a problem. It's not that your church is dead, or that your teachers grade you unfairly, or that your brother picks on you, or that your parents just don't understand you. In fact, it's not really that you *have* problems: you *are* the problem.

It's called sin. Spell that "s - I - n". I can hear some of you now: "Oh, brother, here he goes. This young upstart is going to tell us we're going to hell in a hand basket for all the bad things we've done and for all the dirty habits we have." That, my friend, is where you would be wrong, and if you don't understand what I'm about to share with you, you might even be *dead* wrong.

Some people will tell you sin is drinking, smoking, sex, crime, and a long list of *no-nos*. The trouble with saying this is that you might start believing it's true, and that just because you don't "drink, smoke, cuss, or chew—or run around with girls that do," it means you're not one of those wicked, sinful people with their long hair, drugs, and worldly ways.

As much as I would like to make friends with you, I can't do so at the risk of going easy on the deadly problem we all have. It doesn't matter what we look, act, think, or smell like: ". . . there is no distinction; since all have sinned and fall short of the glory of God" (Romans 3:22, 23 RSV).

So put away your list. These aren't sins; they're symptoms. Sin goes much deeper. And as any good doctor will tell you (and the Great Physician, too), sometimes you can have the disease without showing any of the major symptoms. As Stuart Briscoe relates in *The Fullness of Christ:*

> Sin is an attitude of heart, common to man, which repudiates God's right to possess what He made, control what He designed, and fulfill what He planned. Sin is a cold-blooded rebellion in which rebel man takes the law into his own hands, and overthrows the rule of Sovereign God. Sin is primarily anti-God. . . .

Sin is not something you do wrong: it is something you are. It is a direct confrontation with a loving God who never has wanted to fight with you. Remember God loves us so much that He sent Jesus to die for us.

When you finally realize that sin is nothing less than opposition to God Himself, you can understand that only He can forgive your sins. It would be pretty ridiculous to believe that a man, after sinning against God, could then turn around and forgive himself. Can you imagine having a fight with your best friend, and after you punch him in the nose and he's bleeding all over, you put your arm around his shoulder and say, "That's all right, pal, I forgive me! And I forgive you for getting your nose in the way of my fist!"

Becoming a Christian begins with owning up to your lower nature and allowing God to forgive your sinful attitude of rebellion toward Him. Then after confessing Jesus as Lord and believing in your heart that God raised Him from the dead, God's Holy Spirit takes up residence in your life; and in His eyes, I honestly believe, you become "pure in heart." Consider the witness of God's Word:

> . . . and I will remember their sins no more.

> Hebrews 8:12

He has removed our sins as far away from us as the east
is from the west.

Psalms 103:12

. . . no matter how deep the stain of your sins, I can take
it out and make you as clean as freshly fallen snow.

Isaiah 1:18

For God was in Christ, restoring the world to himself,
no longer counting men's sins against them. . . .

2 Corinthians 5:19

Now can you see the reason for the "happiness" of this Beatitude? If you are a Christian, God has taken your record of sin out
of His files and burned it, forgotten about it, removed it all the
way into outer space, and washed it as pure as snow—in spite of
the fact that all of us deserved His Son's place on the cross
(Romans 6:23).

As a follower of Jesus, this is still another reason to be glad
you're different. You have life, because "He who has the Son has
life . . ." (1 John 5:12 RSV).

If you are not a Christian, you have a rendezvous with death,
because ". . . he who has not the Son of God has not life" (ibid.).

Why put life off any longer? You can get that nature of wrath
that we all inherit changed by being "born again." You were born
the first time by "water" (natural childbirth), but Jesus said:
"Unless one is born of water and the Spirit, he cannot enter the
Kingdom of God. Men can only reproduce human life, but the
Holy Spirit gives new life from heaven" (John 3:5, 6). To choose
for Jesus is a decision you will never regret; to choose against Him,
even by your apathy, is suicide.

The question is often asked, "Is there life after death?"

Jesus answers it plainly, "No. But there's life after birth!"

3
Mind: Your Own Business

When I was just a boy (not that I'm a girl now or anything), my younger brother, Mike, and I used to share a bedroom. It was one of those classy "all-boy" rooms with bunk beds, pennants, posters on the walls, old Wheaties cultures growing underneath the desk, and a DO NOT DISTURB—GENIUS AT WORK sign on the door.

Every night when we went to bed, our parents would always warn us, "Now you kids get right to sleep. No talking—or else!" We usually minded pretty well, because we knew these strict orders had the fastest belt in the Midwest behind them, and Dad really knew how to use it.

But on one historic evening that a certain area of my body can still remember, we reaped exactly what we sowed: *Trouble*—and that starts with *T* and that rhymes with *D*, and that stands for *Dumb*—which is exactly what we were, to provoke our father.

It started out innocently enough. We were whispering, and Mom heard us from the living room.

"Bobby! Mike! I thought I told you kids to be quiet! Now pipe down!"

"Yes, Ma'am," said the top bunk.

"Yes, Ma'am," said the bottom bunk.

We knew she meant business because of the way her voice cracked when it got too high. We knew better than to push it any further.

Have you ever had a *quiet* pillow fight? We tried to keep the noise down, but Mike kept hitting his head on the ceiling. The results were inevitable.

"Bobby! Mike! I thought we told you to go to sleep! One more peep and it's *the belt!*"

I knew that was our last chance. I could feel Dad's vibrations coming right through the wall.

"Yes, Ma'am," from the top bunk.

"Yes, Ma'am," from the bottom bunk.

"Don't you 'Yes, Ma'am me!"

"Yes, Ma'am!"

That was dumb.

The Spirit Counts

It never really bothered me so much when I got a whipping from my father, because I'm sure I deserved more than I got. What bothered me was the way he seemed to enjoy rolling up his sleeves so he could really get into it. It was his sinister smile and the way his eyes got fiery red that really got to me.

In the same manner today, I don't question whether or not I should punish my son. His big problem is that he's so sweet right after I spank him, it makes me want to do it all the time. The important thing, though, is the *spirit* of that discipline. If through loving but firm discipline I succeed in breaking the *will* of my boy, then I have made a friend for life. But if I thoughtlessly break his *spirit*, then I have created a problem for life. Just going through the motions is not enough if the spirit of my actions is all wrong.

That Blessed Curse

"Do not think that I have come to abolish
    The Old Testament laws and the warnings of the prophets.
        No—I came to fulfill them,
            And to make them all come true" (*see* Matthew 5:17).

I have had my fill of the philosophy that since Jesus came with His message of love, we now live in the "Age of Grace," and we don't have to concern ourselves with the Law anymore. What Jesus said was that not even the smallest letter or punctuation mark of the Law would pass away until its purpose was finally achieved. He came to give the Law real meaning.

Now, just because Jesus defends the Law doesn't mean we can glibly say, "Okay, just tell us what Moses said to do, and we'll do our best to get it done." This can't be what Jesus meant, or God would never have allowed the Holy Spirit to write as in James 2:10:

> And the person who keeps every law of God, but makes
> one little slip, is just as guilty as the person who has
> broken every law there is.

If you want to break a circle, all you have to do is break it in one spot. This revolutionary idea was a terrible threat to the religious people of Jesus' day, and it doesn't sit so well with a few people I know today, either.

You can understand their dilemma. They were keeping the "letter of the Law" the best they could, trying hard to be good, self-righteous people. Now this radical, Jesus, comes along and tells them the same thing that didn't win any popularity contests for Isaiah (*see* Isaiah 64:6) over 700 years earlier:

> Your righteousness is as filthy rags,
> And you're guilty of breaking all of the Law,
> Because you're only keeping its "letter"
> And not its "spirit."

John 1:17 helps to clear this up by stating that God gave the Law through Moses, but grace and truth come through Jesus Christ. The word *grace* explains Jesus' substitutionary death for each of us on the cross, as He took upon Himself the death penalty for our breaking the Law. *Truth* means that Jesus came to help us understand the truth about the real meaning of the "do's and don'ts" of the Law, to show us the crucial difference between the spirit of the Law and the letter of the Law.

This gave rise to one of our Lord's strongest attacks on hypocrisy:

"Woe to you, Pharisees, and you religious leaders—hypocrites!
   You are so careful to polish the outside of the cup,
     but the inside is foul with extortion and greed.
"Blind Pharisees!
   First cleanse the inside of the cup,
     and then the whole cup will be clean" (Matthew 23:25).

This crushing blow to false piety is basically saying that what
a person *is* far exceeds the importance of what he *does*. It is so
easy for me to try and hide behind my religious hyperactivity, but
Jesus will not allow it:

". . . you are like whitewashed tombs,
   which outwardly appear beautiful,
     but within they are full of dead men's bones . . ."
   (Matthew 23:27 RSV).

Jesus is not all that impressed with what *I* can do for Him,
because He knows what *He* can do through me. We can be so
busy *doing* that we don't have time to *be* much of anything.

I think we're beginning to realize that Jesus is giving us a strong
dose of spiritual castor oil to clean the cobwebs out of our sanc-
timonious systems. It isn't easy to take, but it is our only chance.
He said, ". . . unless your righteousness exceeds that of the scribes
and Pharisees, you will never enter the kingdom of heaven" (Matthew 5:20 RSV). And before you're too hard on the scribes and
Pharisees, let me remind you that they were just about the finest
people of their day. They didn't keep only the Ten Commandments, they had a list of some six hundred and thirty-three biblical
laws for living that they spent night and day enforcing.

Now Jesus informs us we've got to be even better than these
people. Moses we could take, but Jesus asks too much; this is a
hard thing that He is saying. Does He mean that He wants us to
step up production, doing better and doing more?

The answer to that is an unequivocal *no*, and herein lies the
key that unlocks true Christianity. Jesus wasn't speaking of more
commandments to obey, or more good works to perform. He

knew there were enough of those already, and mankind was finding itself incapable of meeting them all. He spoke of a *new wine* to be put in new wineskins. His novel message of grace and truth couldn't be contained by the old wineskins of empty religious works. It had to be poured into the new wineskins of God's righteousness and salvation; not a status achieved, but a salvation given by grace (Ephesians 2:8).

It looks like Jesus is trying to get us to understand how impossible it is for us to fulfill the Law. He makes the welcome announcement that we can stop playing spiritual Ping-Pong with God, trying to be good enough to earn life over the curse of death. Galatians 3:13 says that Christ has set us free from the curse the Law brings, by becoming a curse for us. When Jesus was lifted up on the cross, He became the fulfillment of a statement made almost 1,500 years before His birth: "Cursed be every one who hangs on a tree" (*see* also Deuteronomy 21:23). That was *our* curse and *our* tree, but Jesus took them. The Law of Moses held that a spotless lamb had to be sacrificed and its innocent blood shed for a man's sin. Centuries later when John the Baptist recognized Jesus, he exclaimed, "Behold, the Lamb of God who takes away the sin of the world" (John 1:29 NAS).

If you are ever feeling inadequate and a bit desperate because the Law has exposed the cancerous condition of your soul, Believer, you can rejoice in the knowledge that the blood requirement of the Law (Hebrews 9:22) has been completed by Jesus. If you want to know what your end of the bargain is, read John 6:28, 29 AMPLIFIED. It's beautiful.

> They then said,
> > What are we to do
> > > that we may be . . . working the works of God?—
> > What are we to do
> > > to carry out what God requires?
> Jesus replied,
> > This is the work . . . that God asks of you,
> > > that you believe in the One Whom He has sent. . . .

Tough Love

Before you get the idea of freeloading on Jesus and taking the grace of God for granted, think carefully about this: 1 John 5:13 says that if you believe in Jesus, you can *know* for certain that you are a Christian. My point is that if *you* know it, so should everybody else! Jesus warned:

"Beware of false teachers
   who come disguised as harmless sheep,
      but are wolves and will tear you apart.
"You can detect them by the way they act,
   just as you can identify a tree by its fruit . . ."
   (Matthew 7:15, 16).

Just because: "There is therefore now no condemnation for those who are in Christ Jesus" (Romans 8:1 NAS), you can't escape the fact that the road to Calvary was *not* an easy one for Jesus. As Bill Milliken, in his book *Tough Love*, quotes George McLeod:

I am rediscovering the claim that Jesus was not crucified in a cathedral between two candles, but on a cross between two thieves, on the town garbage heap, on a crossroad so cosmopolitan that they had to write His title in Hebrew and in Latin and in Greek, or shall we say, in English, in Bantu, and in Africaans—at the kind of place where cynics talk smut, the thieves curse and soldiers gamble, because that is where He died, and that is what He died about, and that is where Christians should be and what Christians should be about. [He died *in* the world, *for* the world.]

There's a world out there, Christian, that needs an example of *peculiar* living and loving. Jesus said, "Blessed are those who hunger and thirst for righteousness . . ." (Matthew 5:6 RSV). We're just not hungry enough to do good, and not thirsty enough to want more. There is an oversupply of used-to-doers, should've-doners, and almost-diders. How about a few abundant-livers? It won't be easy, but Jesus never said it would be. When the going gets tough, the tough get going.

It could be that for too long we've been "talking cream" and "living skim milk." It would help if we believers understood that we haven't been called to a Sunday-school picnic, but a *Crucifixion*. If we stopped wasting our time with bake sales, rummage sales, yard sales, and garage sales—and actually believed that God will take care of our needs if we get down to the business of sacrificial living—then perhaps this world of ours would stop passing Jesus off as a pleasant pastime for good-intentioned people.

Christianity has never lacked for joiners. They're not hard to recruit. Just make sure they get a little red button, a bumper sticker, and a twenty-five-cent certificate, and they'll follow you anywhere. At our team's crusade meetings, when I give the invitation for people to come forward to receive Christ, I ask them to kneel down at the platform. I've heard criticisms of this method, but that's all it is: just a method. The position in which you receive salvation isn't the crucial factor. It's just that I'm willing to put up with all the problems involved if it will weed out those halfhearted people who would "join up" if only they didn't have to kneel down and take a chance on soiling their trousers or being uncomfortable for a moment. If this means that fewer numbers come forward and our reputation as "successful evangelists" suffers, I'm not going to lose any sleep over it. We're not out to see how many scalps we can get. We're recruiting *disciples* for Jesus.

"If any man would come after me,
     let him deny himself
         and take up his cross daily
             and follow me" (Luke 9:23 RSV).

An important word that a Christian should take a long look at and then throw out of his vocabulary is *moderate*, because it is one thing that he can never be in his walk with Jesus. In Luke 11:23 RSV Jesus says, "He who is not with me is against me." Once again the Sermon on the Mount makes it clear:

"No one can serve two masters;
    for either he will hate the one and love the other,
        or he will be devoted to the one and despise the other.
            You cannot serve God and mammon [the world]"
            (Matthew 6:24 RSV).

Just think of it! Jesus, the One who made our salvation possible in the first place, now does His own legwork and becomes our Evangelist, pleading with us to choose Him as our only Lord. He knows the ugly predicament of being pulled between two masters.

Jacob had two wives,
    And it almost ruined him.
        Judas served two gods,
            And the vice he was caught in squeezed him to death.
            Richard Nixon played two roles,
                And suffered the disastrous consequences.

The middle of the fence is too narrow to stay on top of for long. Eventually James 1:8 KJV catches up with you: "A double minded man is unstable in all his ways."

We've been treating Jesus as a passenger instead of as the Pilot; He's been part of the cargo instead of the Captain. The fact is you cannot have sin and the Saviour.

Fruit of the Groom

Not long ago, a friend of mine said to me, "Bob, that pianist in your group is really a born-again Christian."

I acted surprised by the statement (even though I've heard it too many times before). "He's a what?"

"He's really a born-again Christian."

I don't let people get away with that, not even friends. "Do you know any other kind?" I sincerely replied.

"You know what I mean, Bob. He's really committed."

Of course I knew what he meant, but this is too much. We have to stop making distinctions between brands of Christians, even if we start only in our speech. I don't know any true Christians who aren't "born again." I don't know any genuine believers who aren't committed.

The Bible says that I can't be your judge (and vice versa), but I have every right in heaven to be your "fruit inspector." Jesus said in Matthew 7:20 KJV, "Wherefore by their fruits ye shall know them." You should be able to check out my daily activities and see Galatians 5:22, 23 come alive.

> But when the Holy Spirit controls our lives
>   he will produce this kind of fruit in us:
>   love, joy, peace,
>   patience, kindness, goodness,
>   faithfulness, gentleness, and self-control. . . .

That's a pretty tall order, I know, but don't worry: *you* don't have to fill it. That's why all these characteristics are called the "fruit of the *Spirit,*" and not the fruit of Bob Laurent. Just agree with James 2:17 that "faith" is an action word, and realize that the Bible is the only book you possess that is best read "on the run."

It's No Secret

While you are *running* and *doing* all the right things (keeping the "letter of the Law"), make sure that the "spirit" of your actions is genuine. It is at this point that Jesus challenges us all to leave kindergarten behind and get out with the "big kids" where the tough love of Christianity has got to work: the critical battlefield of your thought life. I can hear you now:

"Now, Bob. Wait just a minute! You've stopped writing and now you're meddling. Keep your nosey Bible verses out of my thought life. I mean, isn't anything sacred? Can't a guy have any secrets? I bought this book because I'm concerned about my *actions.* I want to be a better Christian, but what's that got to do with my thoughts?"

Everything, my friend, everything. First of all, you don't have any secrets and you never will. Hebrews 4:13 states,

He knows about everyone, everywhere.
Everything about us is bare and wide open
to the all-seeing eyes of our living God;
nothing can be hidden from him
to whom we must explain all that we have done.

Luke 8:17 tells us (author's paraphrase):

For nothing is secret,
That shall not be made manifest;
Neither is anything hidden,
That shall not be brought to light
And made plain to all.

This is a fairly simple idea, but not until the sheer weight of it finally hit me, did I do some serious changing. I guess I realized that since He knew everything anyway and was going to judge even my secrets, I might as well allow Him to produce something in me that would be worthwhile.

Think Snow

Another reason that God is concerned with your thought-life (and you should be, too) is the profound truth (Proverbs 23:7 KJV): "As a man thinketh in his heart, so is he."

In other words, a man *is* what he *thinks.* Ouch, that hurts! And trying to hide those thoughts doesn't do any good. God already knows them. One of the most powerful Bible verses you will ever read is Hebrews 4:12. Mark this one well (author's paraphrase):

For whatever God says to us is full of living power:
It is sharper than any two-edged sword,
Cutting swift and deep
Into our innermost thoughts and desires
With all their parts,
Exposing us for what we really are.

Now go back and read that verse again. Underline and memorize it in your trusty old King James Version if you want; or your

Amplified, New American Standard, or Revised Standard Version. You can even mark it in your Reversed Standard Vision if you have one. I don't care; just learn it. And every time you start getting a little bit proud of your faith and think that God is pretty lucky to have you on His team, then pull it out and read it again.

Jesus is saying that if you lose the battle on the field of your thoughts, you have lost it altogether. Why? Because He knows that murder is only anger full-grown, and adultery or sexual perversion are really only lust full-grown. No matter how pious we act outwardly (and I'm good at that) or what type of religious mask we wear to cover up, He sees through the tinsel and inspects the heart.

When the Prophet Samuel was out looking for the next King of Israel, he came across Eliab, the older brother of little David. Eliab must have been quarterback for the Bethlehem Bombers or something, because old Samuel was very impressed with his handsome features and beautiful physique.

> But the Lord said to Samuel,
> "Do not look at his appearance
>   or at the height of his stature,
>   because I have rejected him;
>   for God sees not as man sees,
>   for man looks at the outward appearance,
>   but the Lord looks at the heart" (1 Samuel 16:7 NAS).

Jesus informs us firmly that anyone who is just angry with his brother and thereby treats him poorly is in danger of the "hell of fire" (*see* Matthew 5:22 RSV). In that case, it looks like it might be time for some of us to lay down this little book, get up out of our comfortable seats, and go apologize to the people that we've mistreated today.

That reminds me. . . . Just a moment, I'll be right back.

I'm back. Someone told me once to practice what I preach, so I just went and told my wife that I was truly sorry for playing Frisbee with the neighbor boy tonight instead of spending the time that I had promised with her and the kids.

When you've been married for eight years, you don't have to say much to be understood. Our conversation went something like this:

"Honey?"

"Yes?"

"I'm sorry."

"What about?"

"The Frisbee."

"Oh."

"You're not mad?"

"Yes, I am."

"I'm sorry."

"I know."

"I love you."

"I know."

"Then what's wrong?"

"I'm still mad!"

So it didn't work this time, but I still feel better and I'll be able to sleep tonight—*wherever* I sleep tonight!

Jesus said:

"So if you are offering your gift at the altar,
    and there remember that your brother has something against you,
        leave your gift there before the altar and go;
            first be reconciled to your brother,
                and then come and offer your gift"
                (Matthew 5:23, 24 RSV).

You could go to church until people start thinking you're the janitor of the place, but it won't do you any good if you have unjustly hurt another person and done nothing to correct the situation.

Try it right now. Go make things right with that person. It doesn't matter that you don't know what to say, because it won't be you doing the talking anyway. Matthew 10:20 says God will speak through you.

Why not do it now? I'll wait for you. As soon as the shock is over, the person you've apologized to will be your friend again. In fact, after you've cleared the air with him, maybe a chain reaction of honest confession will begin and he'll straighten out a few crooked areas of his life, too. Spontaneous confession and honesty: that's what I call *revival*.

If you need a little motivation on this, just remember that someday you will be appearing before a Higher Court. The Bible calls it the "Great White Throne Judgment" and Jesus will be the Judge (*see* Revelation 20:11). Wouldn't it be better for you if you settled your differences "out of court" right now?

What He Feeds Me, I Will Swallow

"You have heard that it was said,
   'You shall not commit adultery,'
      But I say to you
         that every one who looks at a woman lustfully
         has already committed adultery with her in his heart"
(Matthew 5:27, 28 RSV).

Now the two-edged sword is coming a bit too close for comfort. There are very few of us that the "Sexplosion" hasn't deeply affected. Everywhere we turn—from newspapers to magazines to movies to toothpaste ads—we are confronted with "sexploitation." Add to this the braless look, the see-through look, the miniskirt (or "skimp"), the Pill, and anything else the devil can throw in, and you've got just about as much pressure as a guy's sexual psyche can stand. I know. I'm a guy.

Just consider the facts:

   1. You are living in a world where your daughter can legalize herself in prostitution and make more money than your son with his college degree in engineering.
   2. There are over fifteen million sex magazines read every month by over one-third of the American public.
   3. Over 1,200,000 illegitimate babies are born every year in this country, even with liberalized abortion laws.

4. The average age of the unwed mother in America is thirteen, delivering at age fourteen.

5. Venereal disease and other sexually related diseases have reached epidemic proportions.

It's safe to say, "Sex is on the *loose.*"

Sex is not a dirty word; it has been made that way by dirty minds. The author of that dirt is none other than the original Seducer, who has had centuries of practice in sexual perversion. According to the Bible, God created sex to be beautiful:

> Now although the man and his wife were both naked, neither of them was embarrassed or ashamed.

> Genesis 2:25

But as soon as Adam and Eve chomped down on the fruit of the Tree of Conscience and fell to the conditioning of the world's system, they allowed the devil to tell them what *sex* was. The next thing we read is:

> . . . suddenly they became aware of their nakedness, and were embarrassed.

> Genesis 3:7

Sex is certainly one of Satan's most useful weapons in his age-old scheme to infiltrate the ranks of the Believers. Ever since God put the Church in the world, the Tempter has been trying to put the *world* in the Church. Perhaps that is why Jesus firmly puts an end to any fantasies that we Christians might be entertaining about sex. He says that if we just *look* at a girl lustfully, we've raped her with our minds and gone to bed with her in our hearts. That's strong language and one ultimatum that's always been hard for me to take. But if I piously sing: "Where He leads me I will follow," then my life must also agree that, *"What He feeds me, I will swallow."*

Does Jesus mean that because you can't even look at a girl lustfully, you have to turn in your membership to the G.W.C.A.

(Girl Watcher's Club of America)? Don't forget what He said about your eye being the "lamp of the body." Whatever gets in by the eye winds up in the heart, and Jesus said that out of the heart comes all that is evil (Matthew 15:19).

One Scripture passage that has helped me tremendously in the battle to keep my "eye" clean is Proverbs 4:23–25. It says:

Above all else, guard your affections.
For they influence everything else in your life.
Spurn the careless kiss of a prostitute.
Stay far from her.
Look straight ahead;
don't even turn your head to look.

You can't imagine all the times this thought has come to our rescue. As our team is driving down the road in the Good News Circle "Bread Truck" (*see* John 6:35), one of the guys will spot a slinky-looking girl walking along the right side of the street and quickly yell, "Eyes *left!*" It sure beats running into telephone poles.

Both sexes—especially you girls—could make it a lot easier by watching what fashions you use to decorate your bodies. Next time, before one of you girls puts on a halter top that's going to make guys walk into parking meters when they see you, take a look at Proverbs 11:22. It could revolutionize your dress habits:

A beautiful woman
lacking discretion and modesty
is like a fine gold ring
in a pig's snout.

Kind of has a poetic ring to it, doesn't it? Instead of dressing to "knock a guy's eyes out," why not try dressing as if Jesus were your escort. He is.

You fellows could help things immeasurably too by taking the pressure off your girl friends. Don't make them constantly have to say *no* to you. If her first *no* isn't good enough for you, then the odds are that you're not good enough for her. Remember:

Lust can't wait to *take*,
But love can wait to *give*.
Lust is conquest;
Love is surrender.

Your girl was never meant to be the one who has to say *no*. You're supposed to set the limits. It's always amazed me how a guy will use every girl he meets, and then expect to marry a pure young woman. I've never been one for double standards, and I get a little burned up every time I hear how some *girl* has "gotten herself into trouble."

If all of this sounds prudish to you, then I guess I'm one of the youngest prudes you know. It's just that I have this daughter, you see. Her name is Holly. She's not quite a year old yet, but already I can tell that I'm going to have to give her "ugly lessons" to keep guys from wearing a path to our front door.

I'm looking forward to that first time a boy comes by our house to ask Holly to go out for a Coke (with continuing inflation for fifteen years, that's probably all he'll be able to afford). It might go something like this:

Knock, knock, knock.

I leap to the door and fling it open before the third knock is done. "Hi there, son. What's on your *mind?*"

"Gulp! Uh-h, hello, Mr. Laurent. Is Holly ready yet?"

"No, she's still upstairs combing her hair [if she ever gets any]. Why don't you come on in?"

"Thank you, sir, I will."

He sits down on the edge of our living room couch (if we ever get one) and I pull up a chair right in front of him. We're eyeball to eyeball. "Holly tells me that you're a Christian."

"Yes, sir, I'm a born-again and committed one." (Sound familiar? I'll straighten him out later.)

"That's good. Then you know how to treat her, right?"

"Yes, sir, I do."

"Terrific! Here's ten dollars—buy her *two* Cokes. And remember, no hanky-panky."

"Don't worry, Mr. Laurent. Holly can take care of herself."

"What do you mean?"

"Haven't you heard? She just made first-string fullback on the football team."

"Son?"

"Yes, sir?"

"Let's pray."

Sex Standards

Sex within the confines of a Christian marriage can be a beautiful servant, but sex run through the gutters of this world can be a terrible master. This is a crucial area of your life in which you can be justifiably severe with yourself. You can't play games with sex in your thought-life for long without disastrous consequences. Be holy at all costs. As you can see, this is nothing to be flippant about.

> If your right eye causes you to lust,
> > Gouge it out and throw it away. . . .
> > > And if your right hand causes you to sin,
> > > > Cut it off and throw it away.
> Better for part of you to be destroyed
> > Than for all of you to be cast into hell
> > > (Matthew 5:29, 30 PARAPHRASE).

Here are a few meaningful Scriptures I often share with friends who need guidance concerning sex: 1 Thessalonians 4:1–8; 2 Timothy 2:22; Ephesians 5:1–11. It would be valuable to look these up. To find out what the difference is between true love and cheap lust, study (again and again) the entire chapter of 1 Corinthians 13.

Divorce: The Easy Way Out

Since adultery can lead to divorce, Jesus goes on to say:

> ". . . every one who divorces his wife,
> > except on the ground of unchastity,
> > > makes her an adulteress;

and whoever marries a divorced woman
commits adultery" (Matthew 5:32 RSV).

It is more than likely true that divorce often starts innocently
enough in the thought-life of a married couple. But a person *is*
what he *thinks,* and no matter how naïve the beginning of a
divided family is, the hideous fact remains that there are approximately twenty-five million divorced people in this land of broken
homes. As I stated in my first book *What a Way to Go,* "Messed-
up families produce messed-up children."

It was too easy to get a divorce in the day that Jesus preached
His mountaintop message. All a man had to do if he got upset
with his wife was to say to her, "I divorce thee. I divorce thee.
I divorce thee." That was all. And it's not much harder to get one
today. I heard about a man who filed for divorce on the grounds
of immaturity.

"Immaturity!" exclaimed the judge. "You can't get a divorce
for that. Just what do you mean?"

"Well," said the disgruntled husband, "Every time I get in the
bathtub, my wife has the audacity to burst through the door and
sink my rubber ducky and all my toy boats."

I know of only one foolproof method for you wives to avoid
divorce court—let your example of submission lead your husband
to Jesus.

I know of only one surefire plan for you husbands to make your
marriages work—carry your bride across the threshold of salvation.

This might be a different sort of way to start a marriage, but
then you're a different sort of person.

4
Be Real: Help Fight Truth Decay

I have a friend who doesn't know me. At least I don't think there's much of a chance that he would ever remember meeting me that wonderful day that he spoke at an all-school chapel. I was a first-year seminary student and still learning what should have sunk in during my years at a Christian college: no school—whether it's of the highest calibre or not—can make you into a productive student, let alone a genuine Christian. I needed a lesson in integrity, and that man was about to deliver it "no-holds-barred." He addressed the entire student body, but it seemed that he stared right through me.

"Gentlemen, if you learn nothing else in your three years at this institution—and those years should be rich in knowledge—at least learn to *be real.*"

I sat there under powerful conviction. How did he know I was a fraud? That little two-word phrase began to burn into my mind. *Be real. Be real. Be real.*

The only thing I could hold on to was the fact that maybe our distinguished speaker wasn't so "real" himself. Maybe he just had the knack of capturing an audience's attention and driving home his high-sounding ideals when he actually didn't live that way himself.

But secretly, I wanted to be wrong. I wanted to change. I needed to reach out and touch a flesh-and-blood, involved, dynamic believer. Our visitor appeared to be that, but was he? I had to find out.

My chance came as a surprise. After chapel was over, I was asked by a member of our faculty if I would like to go out to eat with members of the administration and the morning's speaker. Would I ever! Not only did this give me a chance to test out his mettle by asking brilliant and pointed questions, but I was starved, and peanut-butter-on-rye was the only alternative.

I didn't have a chance to doubt him for even a minute. He maintained his electrifyingly candid and humorous ways through the entire predinner conversation. It was none of that cheap, small talk, but deep, soul-searching stuff. Then the food came and I watched him change gears, only to accelerate as he continued to talk about Jesus, coming up for air only when necessary.

"You're a great man," I thought. "You seem to be as down to earth with the elite of our faculty as you were with us students this morning. But I need to know for certain."

No sooner had I secretly expressed my last semblance of doubt than the clincher came. My new friend had been playing "chew and show" the whole meal without knowing it; he talked while he ate, constantly exposing the Chef's Special. The inevitable happened as he reached the climax of his 143rd illustration. A gigantic piece of shrimp flew out of his motorized mouth and landed directly on the right arm of the president of our seminary. I froze. The president, a good-natured man himself—but obviously shocked—just sat there with an I-can't-believe-it look on his stately face. With not a split second of indecision, that beautiful man reached over, plucked the escaped delicacy off the president's suit, and returned it into the "jaws of life," without even breaking stride!

"You're for real, Mr._____. You're for real." At that moment I signed up for a lifetime course in being real myself.

A Piece of Pie-ty

In the Sermon on the Mount, Jesus once again levels off our pride in three important areas of the Christian life: giving, prayer, and fasting.

GIVING: OTHERS NEED IT

"Beware of doing your good deeds publicly, to be admired,
   For then you will lose the reward from your Father in
   heaven" (*see* Matthew 6:1).

Jesus said we should be so humble and discreet about our
giving, that we shouldn't even let our left hand know what our
right hand is doing. But as I see it, our three most common
reasons for giving are:

1. It's tax deductible.
2. It makes me feel good.
3. It gets me recognition.

Although I do itemize my deductions every April 15, and I do
get a warm feeling from giving to others, it's that third reason that
describes my brand of charity so well. When I do a kindness to
someone, I want the world to know about it. If they don't find
out naturally, I make sure they do somehow.

A few weeks ago while Joyce was downstairs taking care of
the kids, I decided to clean the upstairs bathroom spic-and-
span. I like to do something like that—but only once every
two or three years so that it doesn't become just another
monotonous routine.

After I'd finished, it felt good to have done a kindness for my
wife, but that just wasn't enough. The bathroom looked beautiful
—I'd even changed the Ty-D-bol dispenser—and now I needed
recognition.

I marched down the steps and proceeded to do everything
clever I could think of to get her up there to admire my sacrificial
efforts. But she wouldn't go. I know I must have looked like a fool
as I followed her around the house, dropping subtle hints like,
"You don't have to go to the bathroom, do you, honey?"

That type of giving is better left undone. Why do *you* give—
to be admired and praised by your friends? I wonder how many
of us would still give if our names were no longer lifted up
alongside the gift.

Old Ananias and his wife, Sapphira, had this same problem in Acts 5. They wanted praise and flattering looks for their generosity, but their hearts were not right in giving. While they were lying, the Lord was judging their hearts. They were dying to get attention, and Simon Peter obliged them.

This tragic story brings up an interesting theory on New Testament giving that I'm surprised I never hear anyone mention. As first-century believers, Ananias and Sapphira found themselves caught up in a remarkably unselfish group of Christians that didn't exactly emphasize tithing. If you're a pastor this is a subject that is probably close to your heart, since Jesus said that where a man's treasure is, there will his heart be also (Matthew 6:21).

Most clergymen preach tithing for two reasons: (1) it's a good Old Testament concept (Malachi 3:10, 11); and (2) they know they're lucky if they can get their congregations to come across with anything near a tenth of their earnings. Compare this with what the Apostle Paul said in Philippians 3:7, 8 RSV:

> But whatever gain I had,
>   I counted as loss for the sake of Christ.
>   Indeed, I count everything as loss. . . .

It could be that the New Testament way of giving was meant to be the loss of all things into a sort of mutual Christian bank account. Acts 2:44, 45 gives us a clear picture of an amazing little community:

> And all the believers met together constantly
>   and shared everything with each other,
>   selling their possessions
>   and dividing with those in need.

The next time you start complaining about the high cost of being a Christian in the age of inflation, and praying about whether you should tithe on your gross income or just on your take-home pay, remember that you should probably be giving *everything*.

Jesus' words on false piety are aimed at our hearts, not our pocketbooks, because He knows that a man with a regenerated heart will give unreservedly and without seeking empty applause. Don't ever let John 12:43 KJV describe your motive in giving: "For they loved the praise of men more than the praise of God."

PRAYING: GOD NEEDS IT

"And when you pray,
    you must not be like the hypocrites;
        for they love to stand and pray
            in the synagogues
            and at the street corners,
            that they may be seen by men.
        Truly, I say to you,
            they have their reward" (Matthew 6:5 RSV).

I don't believe there is anything that blesses the supernatural heart of God more than His seeing a "peculiar" believer humbly bowed in prayer. But here again, the importance of being real while you pray cannot be overstated.

James 4:2, 3 wonderfully illustrates the two sides of the prayer coin:

You do not have, because you do not ask.
    But even when you ask, you do not receive,
        Because you ask wrongly—
            You want only what will give you pleasure
            (PARAPHRASE).

Praying for Keeps

We Christians are seldom known as "prayer warriors"— "prayer *worriers*" certainly comes closer to the truth. We worry so much about whether God will answer our prayers that we just never seem to get around to asking Him. If we only realized the vast resources available, we might start storming the gates of heaven with our bold petitions instead of making it difficult for

God to get even an anemic "Now I lay me down to sleep . . ." out of us. Matthew 21:22 says:

"You can get anything—
   anything you ask for in prayer—
      if you believe."

And consider this mighty passage from John 14:12–14 RSV:

"Truly, truly, I say to you,
   he who believes in me will also do the works that I do;
      and greater works than these will he do,
         because I go to the Father.
"Whatever you ask in my name,
   I will do it,
      that the Father may be glorified in the Son;
   if you ask anything in my name,
      I will do it."

Do you understand what this suggests? Through prayer you can be so filled with the miraculous power of God that should a mosquito bite you this summer, you will probably hear him fly away singing, "There's Power in the Blood!"

James 5:16–18 declares:

The earnest prayer of a righteous man
   has great power and wonderful results.
   Elijah was as completely human as we are,
      and yet when he prayed earnestly
         that no rain would fall,
         none fell for the next
         three and one half years!
   Then he prayed again . . .
      and down it poured. . . .

When a Christian prays for rain, he should carry an umbrella.

Besides wonder-working power in your life, God promises to supply you with wisdom—a precious commodity in these shallow days.

> If you want to know what God wants you to do,
>   ask him, and he will gladly tell you,
>   for he is always ready to give
>   a bountiful supply of wisdom
>   to all who ask him;
>   he will not resent it (James 1:5).

How many Christians waste years wishing they knew God's will for their lives, when this passage says all they have to do is ask Him. It would save them a lot of worry-filled, sleepless nights. Instead of lying there counting sheep, they could be talking to the Shepherd. If it's important enough for them to worry about, it's important enough for them to pray about.

Never think that your problem is too difficult to bring before God. A friend of mine once told me, "If your problems are long-*standing,* or deep-*seated,* try *kneeling.*" He was right.

Instead of being an also-ran in your prayer life, try proving God out and you'll see Him "open up the windows of heaven for you and pour out a blessing so great you won't have room enough to take it in!" (Malachi 3:10).

Praying *Between the Lines*

Now remember that when Jesus says to us that we're not to pray for the praise of men, He's not delivering a message on ethics. The Sermon on the Mount was meant for His disciples, men who honestly wanted to do right, religious men with high intentions. It wasn't that they weren't praying, but that they were praying "wrongly." They might have been asking all the right things, but doing it in the wrong way.

The Bible says: "The heart is deceitful above all things and desperately wicked . . ." (Jeremiah 17:9 kjv). I know from experience this is true. I have been deceived more than once by my own heart. I remember going to a hospital one day in the Detroit area to visit a sixteen-year-old student who had been almost killed in a freak football accident. We were holding a week of crusade meetings in a nearby high-school auditorium, and some of his classmates asked me if I would go visit and pray with him. As I stood by his quiet bed, flanked on one side by his mother with her tear-streaked face and on the other by an ominous plasma bottle, I realized I was looking at a pathetic shadow of the once virile young athlete. His mother said that he was a Christian and knew he was in good hands. We talked, and then I prayed.

I was too choked up to stay for long, and as I walked out of that room and slowly shuffled toward the elevator, I got mad at myself for not being able to lay my hands on that boy and say, "In the name of Jesus Christ, be whole."

I know now that I wasn't ready for such a happening. Combined with my compassion for the student was a deeper motivation, something like, "If only I had that kind of power, the world would be beating a path to my door. I'd become famous. Everyone would want me to pray for him. There wouldn't be enough room for the crowds at our meetings."

Your own prayer life can be dreadfully dishonest without you ever realizing it, simply because your prayers can sound so good but not have any bona fide content. You must force yourself to be real and get at the true motives behind them. For example, I once heard a father pray,

> Lord, get ahold of my son. Make him a new person.
> Save him, Jesus, and make him Your child.

Now I knew this family's situation very well, and although I could never disagree with the sound of that father's prayer, it could be that it was mostly noise, "a sounding brass, or a tinkling cymbal." Perhaps this prayer had a deeper tone to it, such as:

> O Lord, I don't know what I'm going to do with my son if the "meathead" doesn't straighten out. He's bad publicity for me, and people are beginning to talk. Besides, I never know where he is, or what he's doing. I worry about him, and I think I'm getting an ulcer. Please save him, Lord, and maybe he'll come in before midnight.

Speaking as a young father, my question to any dad is: Are you really concerned about the soul of your son, or is it mostly just your own discomfort that has you on your knees? Are you willing to let the reality of this problem reach you and produce in your spirit a deep sense of personal repentance and *agapē* love for your son. If not, then get ready to lose him, because you will. I'm not concurring with the mistakes your boy has made, but keeping your family together in Jesus should be more important than trying to figure out who's to blame for the problems. Just shut your generation gap and get on with some godly prayer and action. The road to your family's recovery could begin if you would just be real in your caring.

Another prayer we've all heard is,

> Please, Lord, save my husband. Help him to be a good
> Christian man.

This is a wonderful prayer that I have seen God answer many times, but when He doesn't, it might be because the prayer reads between the lines as follows:

> O Lord, You've got to do something with Herbert! He's
> become so mean. I can hardly stand to be around him.
> Maybe if he becomes a Christian, he'll be easier to live
> with and start going to church. It looks nice for a
> husband and wife to go to church together. *You* love
> him, Lord, and *I'll* try my best to change him.

I'm glad God doesn't work that way, or we'd all try to get away with murder. Instead God's answer is: *I'm sorry, dear, but if you love him, I might change you both!*

Yes, the heart is deceitful. I remember one prayer that might not have gotten any higher than the auditorium ceiling. It was after a meeting in West Virginia and I was praying with a teen-aged guy who blurted out an extremely honest request:

> God, please save my parents, so they'll get off my back
> and I can date Linda again.

Do you see now why Jesus is pushing so hard this idea of being real? You may think you're trying hard to be generous and gracious with all your loving acts, but is the real motivation behind your charity the fact that you perform best when the press photographers are there to get your picture and give you a full run of publicity? Why is it that we always want to get the credit? I guess it's just that we want people to know what fine fellows we can be. In fact, I don't think anyone really does know what a truly nice guy I am.

FASTING: YOU NEED IT

"When you fast, don't put on a sad face as the hypocrites do,
   For they disfigure their faces,
      So that all men may see that they are fasting.
         This is the truth I tell you—
         They are paid in full.
"But when you fast, wash your face and put on your festive clothing,
      So that to men you may not look as if you were fasting,
         But to your Father who is in secret,
            And your Father, who sees what happens in secret,
            Will give you your reward in full"
            (Matthew 6:16 PARAPHRASE).

Fasting involves more than just going without food, although this is the most popular idea of it. Personally, I'm thankful that its meaning goes deeper. While attending one of Bill Gothard's Seminars in Basic Youth Conflicts in Chicago, I experienced a feeling of frustration that I'll never forget; it threatened to ruin an otherwise marvelous spiritual experience during the session in which he spoke on fasting.

I was sitting in the middle of a group of four women whose combined weight easily rivaled the entire defensive line of the Chicago Bears football team. They got excited about the idea of "missing a few meals for Jesus," but I could only remember that my theme has always been: "Every Ounce Counts." At 144 pounds soaking wet, I thought that fasting would literally kill me.

I know that being a Christian can be "tons of fun," but some believers carry that a little too far, and go around quoting Leviticus 3:16 KJV: ". . . all the fat is the Lord's."

Of course, biblical fasting can involve going without any unnecessary indulgence, anything that leads to leisure, pleasure, and the delights of the body. Certainly there are times when all of us need to get away and meditate on the love of Jesus and the way it should be changing us. This is an excellent time to fast.

Matthew 4:3 says that Jesus Himself fasted as He prepared for the excruciating ordeal of the temptation in the wilderness by the devil. He showed us that fasting, when done with integrity, can help a man disconnect himself from the demands of his flesh and keep his body under the influence of the Spirit, resulting in power and direction from God and rewarding him with patience and character. Fasting is a sound principle, for it is a common fact that when your body is most disciplined, your mental and spiritual faculties are most alert. I learned this even before I became a Christian. A medical student friend of mine explained this to me, and I tried it by going without food for long periods before taking an exam. The only problem is that I didn't combine enough studying with my "worldly fasting." I never got many answers right, but I was the most alert kid in class!

Although fasting for the right reasons can be very profitable, Jesus is exposing here the dangers of doing it to show everyone else what a superpious person you are, how much more devoted and disciplined you are than others. He tells an interesting story:

"Two men went to the Temple to pray.
    One was a proud, self-righteous Pharisee,
        and the other a cheating tax collector.
    The proud Pharisee 'prayed' this prayer:
        'Thank God, I am not a sinner like everyone else,
            especially like that tax collector over there!
                For I never cheat,
                I don't commit adultery,
                I go without food twice a week. . . .'

But the corrupt tax collector stood at a distance
and dared not even lift his eyes to heaven . . .
but beat upon his chest in sorrow, exclaiming,
'God, be merciful to me, a sinner.'

"I tell you, this sinner, not the Pharisee,
returned home forgiven!
For the proud shall be humbled,
but the humble shall be honored!" (Luke 18:10–14).

There is no room for spiritual pride or ostentation in the Christian life. The first thing I look for in a fellow believer is humility. If he is seeking his recognition from the world, he is forfeiting his reward in heaven and he won't get any false flattery from me.

Four times in Matthew 6, Jesus says something like:

"Don't do your good deeds publicly,
to be admired,
for then you will lose the reward
from your Father in heaven" (Matthew 6:1).

Certainly *giving* is a noble thing to do; and *praying* is a high call; and *fasting* is one of the finest, most austere experiences in the Christian life. But if you want to be certain to lose all of the force behind your good works, then the method is easy: *do it all for show.* Give so that people will like you. Embark on a lengthy fast that will cause sympathetic heads to turn your way. Pray so that people will hear you, and let your prayers become monotonous and general. In contrast:

"Don't recite the same prayer over and over
as the heathen do,
who think prayers are answered
only by repeating them again and again . . ."
(Matthew 6:7, 8).

Now I think Jesus made a pretty clear statement here, and it directly precedes the Lord's Prayer in the Sermon on the Mount. So you tell me why, when we gather together at our churchhouses, do we pull out that Grand Old Prayer and recite it "over and over," and "again and again." Sometimes I honestly believe we think God must have lost His copy! He gave His disciples that Prayer as an example of how to be real in their praying, not something to be rehearsed and repeated by rote.

What an irony it is to lose our heavenly rewards as we try to impress the earthly folk with our spirituality. And what a shame —after we worked so hard to earn them!

GOD IS THE SCOREKEEPER

When I finally started wising up in my childhood, you would rarely hear me announce anything like: "Hey, Dad, Bill's drinking the milk right out of the carton without a glass!" or "Mom, Linda's eating out of the wastebasket again!" or "Mikey flushed my frog down the toilet. Somebody spank him!" The reason I stopped playing the stool pigeon was that Bill, Mike, and Linda were not the only ones who got punished. I usually received a good licking too—just for being a tattletale. My father was teaching me very young something that later on Jesus was to make a part of my Christian faith:

"Judge not, that you be not judged.
    For with the judgment you pronounce you will be judged,
        And the measure you give will be the measure you get.
    And why worry about the speck in the eye of a brother
        when you have a board in your own?
        First get rid of the board.
        Then you can see to help your brother"
        (Matthew 7:1–5 PARAPHRASE).

The Amplified Bible translates the above passage as, "Do not judge, *and* criticize *and* condemn others. . . ." Lurking deep within me is a distinctly critical nature. I say "deep" because it is not the type of thing I want anyone to see. I'm not proud of it, it's just there. I want to be Mr. Nice Guy and have everyone notice my kindness, but there are times when I have a hard time hiding my lower nature. I want to be so critical, to give someone a real tongue-lashing—especially when I run into a person with a large ego problem like mine. But I try to hold back and never attack, because I must at least *act* like a Christian, you know, to keep up the good image.

As you've seen already, the Sermon on the Mount has blown all kinds of holes in that poor strategy. I took Jesus literally when He said that if I was just angry with my brother, I had killed him in my heart. I sat down one day last summer and made up a list of my murders. It took the better part of two sheets of paper. If the FBI could get me for my thought-life, I'd be Public Enemy Number One. And Jesus came to say that it didn't matter how I managed to perform my way around my thoughts, I was a killer. The poisonous attitude of a judgmental character was seething within me, and it still likes to flare up now and then.

Forty Ounces of Pruning

One of the certain things about the Christian life is that you can count on God to grow you up and develop you in a way consistent with His plan. You're the one who chose the narrow road; now He might just have to spank you back onto it periodically. He will chip away at you, mold you, and go about refining your imperfections in his "test tube of fiery trials" until finally He's got you where He wants on that Day when His Son returns.

> There is going to come a time of testing
>   at Christ's Judgment Day
>   to see what kind of material
>   each builder has used.
> Everyone's work will be put through the fire
>   so that all can see whether or not it keeps its value,
>   and what was really accomplished (1 Corinthians 3:13).

This is one of the major reasons you can continue to expect the tribulations promised to you in Romans 5.

Jesus says that He is the Vine, and you and I, as Christians, are the fruit-bearing branches. He goes on to say:

". . . every branch that does bear fruit
  he prunes,
    that it may bear more fruit" (John 15:2 RSV).

Here is the same idea again. God will prune you back until you are in good shape. This is precisely what happened to me one unforgettable Saturday night in Michigan. I was staying with two other fellows on the Good News Circle, Mark and Butch, at our host's home in a Detroit suburb. These two guys had just opened a couple of Cokes and headed upstairs to watch television, and I decided to follow their example. I went to the refrigerator, opened the door, and viewed the limited selection: a bottle of Coke, a half-gallon of milk, and a forty-ounce jar of prune juice. I didn't want the Coke, and I just didn't feel like drinking milk, so I took the prune juice.

I walked into the television room to the sound of good-natured ribbing from my friends: "Bob, don't you know what that stuff will do to you?" "Yeh, Bob, you've got enough there to wipe out a whole regiment!"

"Ha, ha! Very funny," I thought. Who do these guys think they are, my mother? I sarcastically replied in my most critical tone of voice, "I'm a big boy now. I'm old enough to take care of myself."

I guess I felt extremely guilty, because the attention they were giving me and the Bottle was really getting under my skin. As I see it now, I had stepped off the narrow road in at least two areas, and it was only a matter of time before God "climbed my clock." I had been catty and critical in my thoughts toward Mark and Butch, and I had sat down to watch a two-hour movie in direct opposition to the promise I had made God not to spend any more time with the idiot box. I was about to be trimmed back a little so that I could bear more of His fruit and less of my own sour apples.

Have you ever been watching a show that had you so captivated that you almost inhaled your entire box of popcorn? Jules Verne's *20,000 Leagues Under the Sea,* with Kirk Douglas as the star, did exactly that to me—only I didn't have any popcorn. Instead, I polished off the whole forty-ounce bottle in less than ten minutes! Needless to say I paid for my bad attitude and broken promise. God literally pruned me back and gave me quite a lot to think about the next morning when I had to preach in two different services. Those crowds heard a couple of the shortest sermons on record. And, even today, I'm still not straightened out!

Judging From the Way She Looked . . .

In order to trim you back, God will often put hard circumstances in your path to teach you His lessons. This is how He dealt with my critical nature even further one night when I received an unwelcome phone call. I talk a lot about how important it is for us Christians to love other people, but when it comes right down to the difficult business of doing it when I don't feel like it, my love is often "out to lunch."

This particular call came at the exact time I was working on a series of messages from the Sermon on the Mount. I had just been reading in Matthew, "Judge not, that you be not judged," when the phone rang. The voice on the other end of the line was desperate, and I sensed that the caller was on the verge of tears.

"Hello, is this Bob Laurent?"

"Yes, it is. What can I do for you?"

"A friend of mine told me you could help me."

"Whoever told you that is wrong. I can't help you, but Jesus can."

"Yeh, I know, I know. That's what I need to hear about. I've tried everything else. I'm getting a divorce. I'm living a nightmare that I never dreamed could happen to me. I need help."

"You need Jesus. Do you really want help?"

"Oh, yes, I do!"

"Then prove it."

Later on that day, my "caller" became my "visitor," and I knew she meant business. She told me on the phone that she was twenty-two years old and had been married at age eighteen. I expected to find a scared-looking little girl at my front door, but the woman who stood there looked like she could have been a hard forty. She was worn out, beaten down, sloppily dressed, and wearing a cheap, matted-down wig. She came in, sat in a chair facing me, pulled out a pack of cigarettes, and started chain-smoking.

Now smoking is one thing the devil has always used in my life to bring out the impatient, mean streak within me. Cloudy, cigarette-filled rooms used to make me nauseous even before I became a Christian and found out that the Bible calls your body "the home of the Holy Spirit" (1 Corinthians 6:19). The Surgeon General only confirmed my feelings when he started putting his warning at the bottom of every cigarette pack. I've never appreciated going out for a pizza and biting into what tasted more like a rancid cigar because of the polluted atmosphere of the place. More than once I've "lost the victory" around smokers. Now I was faced with the problem in my own house.

My frame of mind for counseling was not the best, but I listened to her unwind a story that shocked me out of my indifference. She told how her little boy was deathly ill, with not much hope for recovery; how her husband was caught in a web of drugs and had recently become a pusher to support his habit; how her own life had degenerated into a living hell in which there seemed to be no escape. She spent her evenings bar-hopping now, moving from one slimy hangout to another in her search to fill the emptiness, and being preyed upon by perverts and used by just about everyone. She swore through the tears that she had no friends, that no one loved her, and that *all* her relatives were sitting in judgment on her. And then she said it: "Thank you, Mr. Laurent, for not judging me. You're the only person I've talked to who hasn't judged me."

It seemed I had just read something a lot like that, and now I felt smaller than my pocket-sized Bible. I could see her now through the eyes of Jesus, and heard His words ringing loud and clear:

> "Why do you see the speck that is in your brother's eye, but do not notice the log that is in your own eye? Or how can you say to your brother, 'Let me take the speck

out of your eye,' when there is the log in your own eye?
You hypocrite, first take the log out of your own eye,
and then you will see clearly to take the speck out of
your brother's eye."

Matthew 7:3–5 RSV

"For I was hungry and you gave me no food,
   I was thirsty and you gave me no drink,
     I was a stranger and you did not welcome me. . . .
". . . Truly I say to you,

When you refused to help the least of these my brethren,
   You were refusing help to me"
   (*see* Matthew 25:42, 43, 45 RSV, LB).

I had just been studying the Sermon on the Mount, and now
its Author was sitting directly across from me in my living room.
This time He is a downtrodden, dejected girl coming to me for
help; tomorrow He'll be a filling-station attendant; the next day
a waitress, a mechanic, a door-to-door salesman, or a member of
my own family.

There is a special place reserved for the self-righteous ones with
their Xerox-copy faith, who refuse to see Jesus in their needy
neighbors. Christ emphatically states:

"Depart from me, you cursed,
   into the eternal fire
     prepared for the devil and his angels"
     (Matthew 25:41 RSV).

It doesn't pay to sit in judgment on those around us. Criticizing
other people requires no brains, no thought, no sense, and most
of all *no love*. I am resolved that my home will be a way station
of *love* for desperate souls who pass by in the night; a sanctuary
of *love* for those driven in by the bitter cold hate of the world;
a sacred refuge of *love* where my family and I can retreat for
spiritual warmth and strength before taking on a malignant, un-
loving universe. I have *loved*, I am *loving*, and I *will love* in the
name of my Lord Jesus Christ.

5
I Love You: Is That Okay?

Tradition has it that back in the thirteenth century, King Frederick II wanted to find out what language a child would speak if he had never heard the spoken word. He chose fifty babies and brought them to his palace where he had nurses take care of just their essential feeding and clothing. They were never cuddled, played with, spoken to, or loved.

The king never discovered what the language would be, because the experiment failed: every baby died!

Every person you know needs to be reached out to and touched by the hand with the nail-scar in it. "What the World Needs Now Is Love"—sweet, Jesus-love. Mankind was aching for a physical manifestation of true spiritual love and a God who could understand their deepest problems and help them do something about them.

This points us to the singular factor that makes Christianity different from the other ten major religions of the earth: *love* that is not from this world. Love invaded our planet when ". . . God showed his great love for us by sending Christ to die for us while we were still sinners" (Romans 5:8). And by His death, this world received its first great Valentine's card, signed in the Blood of the Lamb and saying: I LOVE YOU—JESUS CHRIST.

This is what has always made Christians different as well. "Those Christians," said Celsus in the twelfth century, "love each other even before they're acquainted." One of the wonderful things about knowing Jesus is that you immediately become a member of the most loving fraternity in the world. In our travels with Christ, we find an instant camaraderie and bond of love with fellow believers wherever we go. This is the mark of a true Christian:

> We know that we have passed out of death into life,
>> because we love the brethren.
>>> He who does not love remains in death (1 John 3:14 RSV)

> "A new commandment I give to you,
>> that you love one another" (John 13:34 RSV).

> Pay all your debts
>> except the debt of love for others (Romans 13:8).

> And walk in love,
>> as Christ loved us
>>> and gave himself up for us (Ephesians 5:2 RSV).

> But if a person isn't loving and kind,
>> it shows that he doesn't know God—
>>> for God is love (1 John 4:8).

> "Your strong love for each other
>> will prove to the world
>>> that you are my disciples" (John 13:35).

Now we have hit upon the bedrock of the whole Jesus Movement, the hallmark of Christianity: love. 1 Corinthians 12 deals with the spiritual gifts from God, including faith, healing, wisdom, miracles, prophecy, tongues, and so on, but the thirteenth chapter unmistakably states that "the greatest . . . is love."

If love is the greatest gift a Christian can have, then the greatest problem he can have is a lack of love. Too often we're known as "porcupine Christians"; we've got a lot of good points but nobody can get near us. I believe that the only glue that held the early Church together was *love*. Her members weren't as concerned about membership as they were about fellowship. There was a "Jesus love-in" so powerful that it threatened to bust the first century wide open.

I call for a Christian Renaissance of Holy Love again today.

Not many such revivals have started from a theologian's typewriter, although I believe it is important for us to have a strong theology. During my years in seminary, it was always hard for me to warm up to "The Ground of All Being," "The Divine Other," "The Primordial Totality," or some such Cosmic Force behind the Universe. I guess the Unmoved Mover never moved me very much.

We can experience the revival so many of us have been praying for when we decide to "Be kindly affectioned one to another with brotherly love; in honour preferring one another" (Romans 12:10 KJV). But what will make us really start caring for each other? Listen carefully:

> . . . see that ye love one another
> with a pure heart fervently:
> Being born again . . . (1 Peter 1:22, 23 KJV).

There's that new-birth thing again. It means that after receiving Jesus Christ as Lord and Saviour, your old nature of selfishness will be replaced with a brand-new nature of loving concern. You can then begin "in honour preferring one another," which simply taken means that you should get out of the way and think more highly of others than of yourself.

Reddy to Love

My wife came home one evening with a mischievous glimmer in her eye after a humorous shopping experience. Joyce told me she overheard two women arguing about whether or not she was actually Helen Reddy. She playfully acted proud of her resemblance to a real, live celebrity, but she wasn't sure just who Helen Reddy was. I informed her that she was a popular representative of the Women's Lib movement, and that she was best known for her song, "I Am Woman."

"Well, how does the song go?" Joyce asked.

I felt a bit annoyed and slightly foolish as I weakly sang the chorus for her, *"I am strong, I am invincible. I am woman.* There

—now let's forget about it. I like you just the way you are."

She chuckled, but didn't lose the glimmer.

I thought I was done with her charade and retired to the bedroom to get some sleep and repress the whole thing.

I should have known better. I tease Joyce so much, and now that the tables were reversed, she wasn't about to let me off the hook so easily. I lay there in bed and heard her humming and clearing her throat out in the hallway. I could tell that any second she was going to make her grand entrance singing "I Am Woman," and watch me do a slow burn. The only thing that saved me was that she's not very good at remembering the lyrics to songs. She strutted into the bedroom, threw her head back cockily, and sang out at the top of her lungs, "I am strong, I am *dispensable.* . . ."

I quickly blurted out as I fell off the bed laughing, "You said it! I didn't!"

After we dried each other's tears from ten solid minutes of uncontrollable laughter, we came to the conclusion that her "mistake" should be a statement made purposely by every Christian who wants to follow Christ's example in loving others. It's not easy to sing, "I'm *not* strong: I am *dispensable*" when the world has taught you that you've got to walk all over people on your self-confident journey through life. And this is the reason that Jesus asks more than most folks are ready to give. He says:

"You have heard that it was said,
   'An eye for an eye and a tooth for a tooth.'
     But I say to you,
     Do not resist one who is evil.
        . . . if any one would sue you
          and take your coat,
          let him have your cloak as well;
       and if any one forces you
          to go one mile,
          go with him two miles.

Give to him who begs from you,
  and do not refuse him
    who would borrow from you" (Matthew 5:38–42 RSV).

I am firmly convinced that Christianity should never present an *intellectual* problem to the nonbeliever. It is a reasonable faith, a rational philosophy of life based upon volumes of empirical, historical evidence. But it will always present a *moral* problem to the follower of this world's ways. It is hard to "turn your cheek," when your background has conditioned you always to stand up for your own rights. Jesus goes even further:

"You have heard that it was said,
  'You shall love your neighbor and hate your enemy.'
    But I say to you,
      Love your enemies
      and pray for those who persecute you,
      so that you may be sons of your Father who is in heaven;
        for he makes his sun rise on the evil and on the good,
        and sends rain on the just and on the unjust.
      For if you love those who love you,
        what reward have you?
        Do not even the tax collectors do the same?
      And if you salute only your brethren,
        what more are you doing than others?
        Do not even the Gentiles do the same?
    You, therefore, must be perfect,
    as your heavenly Father is perfect"
(Matthew 5:43–48 RSV).

Now that's got to be one of the most impossible things you've ever heard, right? I mean how can anyone be expected to love his enemies?

I've never heard anybody explain it like this before, but I have a hunch that one reason Jesus made that challenging statement is that, other than the devil and his unholy legions, He never had any enemies. As He hung on that Cross outside of Jerusalem, suspended for three hours between His true home in heaven and the scene of His execution on earth, He could have summoned ten thousand angels to annihilate His enemies. But seen through the veil of His Blood, the very ones who murdered Him became potential "children of the Kingdom," and He could plead instead, "Father, forgive them, for they know not what they do . . ." (Luke 23:34 KJV).

I believe it has always been closest to God's heart that His enemies become His children, and His children grow up to lead others His way. Please remember the next time you're making out your own list of enemies that you should be seeing them just as Jesus does, as possible brothers and sisters reachable for the Kingdom. Don't waste your time striking out against other people who do you wrong; hit at the source of the trouble. Ephesians 6:12 says you shouldn't be:

> . . . fighting against people made of flesh and blood,
> but against persons without bodies—
>   the evil rulers of the unseen world,
>   those mighty satanic beings
>   and great evil princes of darkness
>   who rule this world;
> and against huge numbers of wicked spirits in the
> spirit world.

Save your punch for the devil. Besides, he's more fun to fight anyway.

> . . . for he who is in you is greater
> than he who is in the world (1 John 4:4 RSV).

Resist the devil
> and he will flee from you (James 4:7 RSV).

The reason the Son of God appeared was
> to destroy the works of the devil (1 John 3:8 RSV).

Try Love for A Change

As I see it, there are several good reasons for loving your enemies:

1. The Bible says that you should.   As far as I'm concerned, God's Word is the final word on the subject. But please don't love me only because John 15:12 says,

"I demand that you love each other
as much as I love you."

I can usually spot those visible few who say they love me "under orders" simply so that they can reach heaven, but secretly are waiting until they get there to come up and bend my halo a little bit, or step on one of my wings.

2. Loving your enemies will be much better on you in the long run. Jesus says,

"Blessed are the merciful,
for they shall obtain mercy" (Matthew 5:7 RSV).

"Your heavenly Father will forgive you
if you forgive those who sin against you . . ." (Matthew 6:14).

The corollary to this, of course, is that if you are not a forgiving person, neither will God forgive you from the death penalty you deserve. Remember, "the measure you give will be the measure you get" (Matthew 7:2 RSV). Therefore, it only makes sense that you "bless those who curse you."

Every once in a while I read something that has a radical effect on my life. At the time I came across S. I. McMillen's book *None of These Diseases,* I was having a terrible struggle trying to love one of my "enemies." Now I know that I probably was more than half of the problem, but back then I honestly believed I was the good guy with the white hat, and this person was the villain. Still, my supposed lack of blame in the matter didn't help me one iota in building any kind of inner peace. I couldn't sleep nights; the contention between us seemed to fill my every thought. I felt like I was getting an ulcer. Then I read this beautiful gem from McMillen, a practicing medical doctor:

> The moment I start hating a man, I become his slave. I can't enjoy my work any more because he even controls my thoughts. My resentments produce too many stress hormones in my body and I become fatigued after only a few hours of work. The work I formerly enjoyed is now drudgery. Even vacations cease to give me pleasure. . . .
>
> The man I hate hounds me wherever I go. I can't escape his tyrannical grasp on my mind. When the waiter serves me porterhouse steak with French fries, asparagus, crisp salad, and strawberry shortcake smothered with ice cream, it might as well be stale bread and water. My teeth chew the food and I swallow it, but the man I hate will not permit me to enjoy it. . . .
>
> The man I hate may be many miles from my bedroom; but more cruel than any slave driver, he whips my thoughts into such a frenzy that my innerspring mattress becomes a rack of torture. The lowliest of the serfs can sleep, but not I. I really must acknowledge the fact that I am a slave to every man on whom I pour the vials of my wrath.

The price of his book is worth it for that one page alone. Nothing short of self-imprisonment can come from a hateful heart. The only way you can free yourself from this cage is not only to forgive the one you've hated, but to *love* him now as well.

3. Loving your enemies is the best way I know of to make them your friends.   Jesus had many weapons from which to select in His fight-to-the-death with sin, and He chose the most powerful one of all: *love.* Love changed the Cross from a heinous emblem of murder and death to the beloved symbol of life that we now wear about our necks and make the subject of beautiful music. I have seen love change a callous, hardhearted nature into a gentle, compassionate spirit. I have seen love change pride to humility, arrogance to kindness, skepticism to belief, lust to purity, and emptiness to abundance. Love is changing me.

4. If you love your enemies you will evangelize them. You will share with them the Good News that Jesus Christ came to give them life, and now they, too, can escape the jaws of hell to live forever in the joy of God's salvation. You can stop guarding an empty tomb and walk away from it bearing witness to the real presence of the Risen Christ.

There's No Excuse

The whole theme of this book is that you, Christian, need to be *different* because the world desperately needs you to be that way. You are not only a precious commodity as this world's "light," but you are its "salt" as well. Without you, the earth has no flavoring, no standard for truth, no meaning in life. I plead with you to come out of your bulb factory and leave your salt-shaker behind—and begin communicating your faith to others.

I honestly believe that if you have been a Christian for any length of time at all, and you have never lifted your voice, your pen, or your carcass from its comfortable pew, to win the "lost" for Jesus, there is a good chance that your religion is phony and your testimony empty verbiage. I know I sound a little merciless and hard-boiled right now, but it's not a pleasant thought to me that vast numbers of potential Christians are dying without ever having been introduced to Jesus. And some of these are members of your own family. While so many of us sit around waiting on some kind of supernatural summons to evangelize, the job is quite frankly not getting done. We don't need a *voice;* we've already got a *verse:* "Go ye into all the world, and preach the gospel to every creature" (Mark 16:15 KJV).

There is a silent majority in the Christian rank and file that must be heard from soon, or it may never gain a hearing again. The world is waiting, but not for long. The command to *go* is as simple as A-B-C; the problem is we are D-E-F.

I have recognized four recurring excuses for not witnessing, that I would like to expose. I've dedicated my life to fighting these and the lies from hell that provoke them:

1. *"It's not my job. I'll let the professional Christians witness."* The fact that I got my "union card" from a seminary and subsequently turned pro is not what makes me an evangelist. On the contrary, the call to witness took no time at all. The moment I said *yes* to life in Christ, I became His ambassador, a fellow-herald of glad tidings with every other believer. Jesus preached:

"Blessed are the peacemakers,
    For they shall be called sons of God" (Matthew 5:9 NAS).

Please do not misinterpret this Beatitude by saying, "Okay, if I decide to be a peacemaker, then I'll be called a son of God." Not so. If you claim to be a Christian, John 1:12 states that you *are* a son or daughter of God, and if you are His child, then you must be a peacemaker. You don't have to be a spiritual Matt Dillon keeping noses clean around Dodge City, or a Henry Kissinger trying to get the Arabs and Jews at least to talk to one another. You see, we're not as concerned here with reconciling men to each other as with reconciling man to God. If a person loves and honors God, then he will love and honor his neighbor, who is created in God's image (Genesis 1:26). The Bible says that after we believed on Jesus and became new creations:

. . . God . . . reconciled us to Himself through Christ,
    and gave us the ministry of reconciliation
    (2 Corinthians 5:18 NAS).

We have the privilege of urging everyone to come into His favor and be reconciled to Him. Before Jesus Christ, you and I were troublemakers; now we are peacemakers. There are several important passages of Scripture supporting the idea that witnessing is your responsibility and privilege.

So faith comes by hearing,
    And hearing by the preaching
        Of the Good News of Christ
        (Romans 10:17 PARAPHRASE).

Often I am moved in one of our meetings to realize that if just a small portion of the large crowd assembled would take this business of witnessing to heart, the sky would be the limit. I can hear Jesus pleading:

"The harvest is so great,
And the workers are so few.
Pray to the Lord of the harvest
And ask Him to recruit more workers
For His harvest fields" (*see* Matthew 9:37).

The Good News Circle could use some help. The harvest field is too big for us. It's easy to get tired and lost in it. There's a commercial going around that says, "The Marines need a few good men." We need a *few good helpers.* As we work together, you can count on the promise that "anyone who calls upon the name of the Lord will be saved" (Romans 10:13). What catalyzes me into action, though, is this verse:

But how shall they ask him to save them
unless they believe in him?
And how can they believe in him
if they have never heard about him?
And how can they hear about him
unless someone tells them? (Romans 10:14).

You are that *someone.*

For you must teach others those things
you and many others have heard me speak about.
Teach these great truths to trustworthy men
who will, in turn, pass them on to others
(2 Timothy 2:2).

One Biblical statement that has always bothered me is:

"When I say to the wicked,
'O wicked man, you will die!'
and you don't tell him what I say,
so that he does not repent—

that wicked person will die in his sins,
   but I will hold you responsible for his death"
   (Ezekiel 33:8).

The New American Standard translates this as, ". . . but his blood I will require from your hand." This is pretty strong language and must be the reason Paul makes certain to announce in Acts 20:26, 27:

"Let me say plainly that no man's blood can be laid at my door,
   for I didn't shrink from declaring all God's message to you."

It is interesting to me that after Jesus charged His disciples with:

"Follow me,
   and I will make you become
     fishers of men" (Mark 1:17 RSV),

the disciples took this responsibility so literally that they made the sign of the *fish* and not the *Cross* the major symbol of their young movement.

Being closely involved with a music ministry, I have had the opportunity to work with many songwriters, but none quite like my good friend and teammate Doug Howell. Mark that name well, because you will hear it again. I say this not just because Doug is musically a creative genius, or that he has one of the finest vocal and keyboard interpretations around. No, the reason his name and work will become known by Christians everywhere is that he combines his talents with an intense desire to be that "peculiar" person that God is seeking to use. Doug is the type that you don't mind complimenting, because he never hears your "snow job." He guards his words carefully and expects you to do the same. The reason for this is his awareness of Matthew 12:36, 37 RSV:

"I tell you, on the day of judgment
   men will render account for every careless word they utter;
     for by your words you will be justified,
       and by your words you will be condemned."

Doug doesn't talk much, so he makes sure that his speech counts for something. This is why he spends most of his time telling people about Jesus. Perhaps my favorite song that he has written is called "I Just Want to Talk About Jesus." It starts off by saying:

Don't make me talk about weather.
    Don't make me talk about trends.
        Don't ask my opinion of the latest styles.
            Can't we talk about something
                That's never gonna end?

I feel the same way. If my every word is going to be judged by God someday, I might as well spend them for eternity and share the love of Jesus.

A few months ago, I decided to take God up on something He said through King David almost three thousand years ago:

Sing a new song to the Lord!
    Sing it everywhere around the world!
        Sing out his praises! Bless his name.
            Each day tell someone that he saves (Psalms 96:1, 2).

It's one thing to sing and preach from the stage, but the great equalizer is witnessing one-on-one in daily life. There have already been many times when I haven't felt like keeping my promise to God, but the results and rewards have been more than worth it.

2. "But, Bob, it's easy for you to witness. You're an outgoing person. I'm kind of soft-spoken and it's just not like me to talk about my faith. I just don't have the personality." This is perhaps the poorest excuse because it denies the central claim of the Gospel: the Holy Spirit can not only change your nature, but He can accomplish His work through *anyone*. I don't care if you're an *introvert, extrovert,* or *pervert,* the Spirit of God can make you a *convert* to Jesus and subsequently a soul-winner.

Moses must have thought that he didn't have the right personality to lay the Word on ol' Pharaoh. He pleaded with the Lord,

"I'm just not a good speaker.
    I never have been, and I'm not now,
        Even after you have spoken to me,
            For I am slow of speech and slow of tongue"
        (*see* Exodus 4:10).

Then Jehovah asked him,

"Who made man's mouth?
    Isn't it I, the Lord?
        Now go ahead and do as I tell you,
            For I will help you to speak well,
                And I will tell you what to say" (*see* Exodus 4:11).

What this and a host of other Scriptures tell me is that I don't have to worry about any lack of innate qualities that would help me in witnessing. My biggest task is to let God out of the box that I regularly assign Him to, and allow Him to do what He does best: convince people of His truth, goodness, and love.

I believe that if all the early apostles could have selected one theme verse for their evangelistic outreach, they would have echoed Paul's words: "For me, to live is Christ . . ." (Philippians 1:21 AMPLIFIED). Notice that it is not "Christ*like*," but Christ Himself. With all due respect to a wonderful old hymn, it's not that "He walks with me, and He talks with me." The truth is even better than that: Jesus walks *through* me, and He talks *through* me. Witnessing becomes so much easier when we get out of the way of the One who's been doing it for hundreds of years. When you think about it, one of the most effortless things in the world for a Christian to do is to witness to his faith in Christ, because Jesus is naturally bound to tell others about Himself better than we ever could.

A friend of mine is always reminding me that we're like the trees that Jesus mentions: ". . . every sound tree bears good fruit" (*see* Matthew 7:17 RSV). It doesn't say that a tree has to sweat, struggle, and strain to produce that fruit; it does it in the natural course of being a sound tree. When is the last time you passed an apple orchard and heard an exhausted apple tree grunting out a loud, "C'mon, apples!"?

This doin'-what-comes-naturally approach reminds us that door-to-door witnessing is definitely not the only method of evangelizing the lost, nor is it always the most effective. With Jesus in the driver's seat, your immediate friends and family become a ready target for God's love. The wonderful thing about an exciting, living faith is that it's *contagious.*

Let me tell you a beautiful family Christmas story that might help you witness "in season and out." There are no elves or flying reindeer or talking snowmen in this story, but there is a Ghost involved here: a Holy One.

A few winters ago, Joyce and I stood outside our townhouse and claimed our community for Jesus, knowing that our prayer triggered God's Spirit into action. We had also been painfully aware that if genuine Christian love was not evident in our own family and the neighborhood, we might as well forget about attempting to reach people out in the world of our crusades and Jesus rallies. First Jerusalem, next Judea, then the whole world as in Acts 1:8.

We don't do as many meetings as we probably should in the area where we live, but imagine my surprise one night last month when I looked up during the invitation and saw all of the members except one of my next-door neighbor's family, on their knees weeping, smiling, and wanting to receive Jesus as Lord and Saviour. Only the father sat in the back, watching with great interest. But in his own words a few days later, he told me, "Bob, what am I going to do with my family? All they talk about is Jesus and *love.* All they do is read their Bibles. I don't have a chance!" And he didn't!

The theme song for his wife, three teen-age sons, and twelve-year-old daughter was, "Sooner or later, love is gonna get ya." This man is now my Christian brother and we're not just next-door neighbors anymore. We have the same address: "heavenly places in Christ Jesus" (Ephesians 2:6 NAS).

And in my enthusiasm, all I can say is,

God is great,
  God is good,
    God lives in my neighborhood.

3. *"I'm afraid to share the Gospel. I mean, what if I go up to someone, and he offers me a knuckle sandwich for my efforts?"*

Have you ever noticed that when it comes to the least element of personal risk, we let our imaginations run wild? When is the last time you picked up the evening paper and read a headline like: JOHN JONES GUNNED DOWN WHILE WITNESSING TO NEIGHBOR?

Of course, just because you possess the Answer to this world's problems, that doesn't mean you will be welcomed by her people with open arms. Remember: "You are the salt of the earth" (Matthew 5:13 RSV), and when salt gets into the wounds of the world, it will sting enough to get a few folks really irritated. There will always be those who don't appreciate "light" and "salt," even when death hangs in the balance. John 3:19, 20 RSV informs us:

"And this is the judgment,
  that the light has come into the world,
    and men loved darkness rather than light,
      because their deeds were evil.
        For every one who does evil
          hates the light. . . ."

For the story of the cross
  Is sheer absurdity to those who are perishing
  (*see* 1 Corinthians 1:18 AMPLIFIED).

To those who are perishing,
  We Christians seem a fearful smell
    Of death and doom (*see* 2 Corinthians 2:16).

It is a well-known fact that you can't always give a young child just what he wants. Instead, you give him what he needs. If I let my son have his way, he would have chocolate ice cream and soda pop for every meal (and so would I). God the Father offers us what we need to gain eternal life, not necessarily what we want.

When you are criticized and abused for carrying His message of reconciliation, pull out Matthew 5:11, 12 RSV and believe it:

> "Blessed are you when men revile you and persecute you
>   and utter all kinds of evil against you falsely on my account.
>   Rejoice and be glad,
>   for your reward is great in heaven,
>   for so men persecuted the prophets
>   who were before you."

You have nothing to be afraid of; it doesn't matter who is against you if God is for you (Romans 8:31). This courageous devil-may-care-but-you-don't attitude can be a springboard to power and miracles in your witnessing. I received an object lesson on this from my son one night deep in the mountains of Tennessee.

Smoky Mountain Breakdown

It was about 9:30 P.M. The four of us sat in the dark of our trailer, waiting out a heavy rain that had started about three hours earlier. Joyce had just gotten the baby to stop fighting sleep, but I wasn't having nearly as much luck with Christopher. It was as if he knew that the day's excitement was far from being over. Besides, he always likes to have his treat before bed, and the cooler with all our food was still on the picnic table, imprisoned there by the rain that separated us.

Finally, the only sound we could hear was the trees spilling their own leafy raindrops. I decided to go for the cooler, grabbed my flashlight, and stole quietly out the trailer door.

There was a deathly silence in the campsite, and the eerie light that I brought to it only added its weird effects to the already intimidating scene. I resolved to make a bold beeline for the table, sweep up the cooler, and be back in the warmth of my bed before you could say "Boris Karloff."

Almost as soon as my mad dash got under way, I was forced to freeze in my tracks. Standing about three feet away in the darkness was the large figure of a man hulking over the cooler. I assumed it was a man because I've never known any woman that big, and I figured he was just passing through our camp on his way to the restroom. I cautiously reached my hand out to him and said, "Sir? Sir?"

Try to imagine my fright when he responded with a deep growl, raised up to his full height as he turned around, and revealed to me the battle-scarred face of an enormous old hungry black bear! If I described him to you from the impression he left on my memory, you'd never buy it. I mean, who'd ever believe a twenty-four-foot-tall saber-toothed bear with fiery red eyes, and satanic horns crowning his massive head. But one thing I know for certain: he was *big* and *ugly,* and I was *scared.* I said something courageous, like "Take the cooler, bear! Take the trailer—take my wife! Take anything you want. It's all yours!"

Just as my petrified mind became aware that my family had been watching this heroic effort to protect them, I heard Christopher's proud battle cry pierce the night air, shocking both me and our uninvited guest:

"Go get him, Daddy-y-y-y!!!"

The bear lumbered away, startled by the boy's shout and probably annoyed that he'd lost his evening snack. I thought to myself, "You want him so badly, Christopher, *you* go get him!"

But that's just the point. If I had allowed my son out of the trailer, I know he would have walked right up to that bear and slugged him in the kneecap. Why? Because he hadn't learned yet to be afraid of bears, or that it was impossible for a little boy to attack a prowling bear. I'm thankful that I hadn't taught him that lesson yet, because if it hadn't been for the undaunted cheer he gave his daddy, that starving animal and I would probably still be squared off over the cooler.

I'm glad that no one convinced young David to be afraid of giants, and that Goliath was too much of a mismatch for his puny slingshot. This is the same position that you can be in as you witness for Christ. Don't ever get to the spot where you have learned to be afraid of telling others about God's love and that it's just not sophisticated to be excited about sharing your faith.

Jesus said He would "never leave you or fail you" (*see* Hebrews 13:5).

For whatever is born of God
    overcomes the world . . . (1 John 5:4 RSV).

"And I have given you authority
    over all the power of the Enemy . . ." (Luke 10:19).

Remember as you live this "peculiar" life that there are three hundred and sixty-five "fear nots" in the Bible. That's one for every day you share Jesus this year.

4. "I get too embarrassed to witness. I guess I care a lot about what others think of me."   The number-one rule in a long list of things to do so that you'll never lead anyone to Jesus is: be concerned more with your own popularity and comfort than you are with the eternal destiny of others.

We Christians cannot afford to get so otherworldly—spewing out spiritual rhetoric and calling nonbelievers heathen and pagan —that we forget they are valuable people and that Jesus died for them as well. They have faces and names. You touch them and they touch you every day. They are members of your family; your parents and children; your best friend at school; your boss; or that wonderful kid from next door who carries your groceries in every Saturday morning.

People are dying at the rate of eighty-three per minute, and that's one hundred and twenty thousand per day. The Bible says:

And it is appointed unto men once to die,
    but after this the judgment . . . (Hebrews 9:27 KJV).

If we really believed this, our concern would accelerate remarkably. I guess nothing seems quite so far away from us as death— until it happens. And then there is nothing closer.

When Death Can Sting

In the "summer of '61," I played on a Pony League baseball team in Springfield, Illinois. My dad was one of the coaches, so

I got to play a lot. One day a thirteen-year-old guy tried out for the team. He looked like an undergrown Huckleberry Finn in a ball uniform, with his baggy pants and shaggy blond hair shooting out from under his cap. I liked him, but not once did I invite him to go with me to church on Sunday night after a game. Sure, I was president of my youth group and you would think that I would have appreciated his attendance and fellowship. But the risk of having him think I was "religious" stood in the way every time I considered witnessing to him. Besides, what if the other guys on the team found out that I was a Christian? Why, they'd probably think that I played with Barbie Dolls and jacks, too.

Six years later at a Christian college where I was playing on the school baseball team, I got my second chance to tell him about Jesus, a chance that so often never comes. There he was in right field again—just like old times. He'd changed a little; he was bigger and more independent, but he still had that ready smile and infectious humor. I liked him. However, even though I was looked on as some kind of spiritual leader at that school, I wasn't about to share my faith in Christ with him. I had never changed; I was still too embarrassed. Maybe he would think I was peculiar or something.

They say that "the third time is a charm," but I know for a fact that it never arrives on time. A few months ago I came home after a long trip, exhausted, but anxious to tell my wife about all the people I had reached for Jesus. Instead she met me at the door and told me about one I hadn't. She informed me that my old friend whom I had failed twice had just drowned in Lake Springfield, not far from my boyhood home. He left behind a beautiful wife, and darling little girl. I still liked him, but now it was too late—*Once to die, and then the judgment.*

For anyone to be embarrassed or self-conscious at the thought of telling others about Christ shows a terrible misconception of what is going to occur before the judgment throne of the Lord.

I saw the dead, great and small,
   standing before [the throne of] God;
      and The Books were opened,
         including the Book of Life.
And the dead were judged
   according to the things written in The Books,
      each according to the deeds he had done. . . .
And if anyone's name was not found
   recorded in the Book of Life,
      he was thrown into the Lake of Fire
      (Revelation 20:12, 15).

Jesus said that there will be "weeping and gnashing of teeth" in the outer darkness reserved for the ungodly, but I have a strong feeling that my own tears will join their flow when I see the people turned away from the throne whom I had opportunity to reach but was too embarrassed to do.

I don't care what your strategies are, or whose plan you're following, or what "Ten Easy Steps to Successful Soul-Winning" book you've been reading. *Just do something.* Make a move. At least show that you have a spiritual pulse. Yes, maybe you will appear to fall flat on your face, but God's Word always bears fruit. It will never return to Him void. He says, ". . . . It shall accomplish all I want it to, and prosper everywhere I send it" (Isaiah 55:11).

Hurry Them *Up*

I heard a story once that all the legions of hell were called together one day by their evil leader, Satan himself. His Infernal Majesty was in a bad mood, as usual, but this time he was boiling mad because too many people down on earth were being won over to his archenemy, Jesus.

Satan thundered to his troops that he had assembled them for an all-important, unholy purpose. He demanded that one of them give him a master plan to put a stop to worldwide Christian evangelism.

One demon immediately stepped forward and proudly hissed

his wicked suggestion: "Ssssire, I have a plan that cannot fail. Let me go to earth and whisssssper in man's ear that *there is no heaven.* When he hears that, he will have nothing to look forward to, and will give up in despair."

There were no cheers for this devilish scheme. It had been tried before by many "good-intentioned theologians," and had never had the results that Satan was looking for now.

A second demon came out of the ghoulish mass and proposed, "Your Majesty, I have a surefire strategy that I'm certain will work. Let me go to earth and reveal to man's mind that *there is no hell.* When he hears that, he will have no reason to live a holy life or to recruit others for such."

It was another good try, but somehow it just wasn't enough for "Old Scratch." The vile assembly of the rulers of darkness still wasn't pleased.

Then suddenly, slithering from out of the mist, came the most clever demon of all. Satan seemed to be listening now for the first time. The evil spirit spoke carefully and allowed every word to fall slowly from his forked tongue, "Our father, who art in hell, hallowed be thy name. There is only one way to bring a halt to man's witnessing about you-know-who. Let me go to earth and tell him that *there is no hurry.*"

And the Prince of Evil rose to lead his contemptible followers in great applause before they went to work to institute this new plan.

My friend, it's working. It's working. We are in a race against time, and our apathy is the spoon that feeds the depths of hell itself. The last thing that Jesus did on earth was to lead a sinner to Himself. Make it the first thing that *you* do today. I don't care how you do it. Let Jesus worry about that. All you have to do is witness in the power of the Holy Spirit and leave the results up to God. Share His love everywhere you go and with everyone you meet.

People are *dying* to know Him.

6
A World of Difference

Let me take you back thirty-five hundred years to a volatile area of the world that is still making headlines today. You're traveling with Moses, wandering through the wilderness with a couple of million people and animals. You've just crossed the Red Sea in a thrilling escape from the Egyptian Pharaoh's chariots, and you're all excited about a God who gives bread from heaven and makes quail fall down at your feet when you're hungry. You start thinking, "God must be real—look at those miracles He's worked."

Then your leader, Moses, comes to you and says, "My children, I must leave you and go to the top of the mountain. God wants to speak with me."

But while Moses is receiving ten of the greatest thoughts in the history of theology, trouble rears its ugly head back down at the campsite. You and your friends are tired of waiting for Moses to come back.

"Hey, Aaron, didn't Moses leave you in charge?"

"Yes, my friend, you know that he did."

"Well, we're bored stiff. How about some action?"

You and the others are too much for the substitute leader, and Aaron gives in to the pressure. If the rest of the story were happening today—and I believe it is—it might go something like this. . . .

God's Frozen People

The daily miracles that God has been springing on you are not enough. You need more. Besides, all this "wilderness wandering" is getting old fast; bumper-to-bumper camels all the way. You've got Excedrin headache number forty and you just need a little relaxation. It's not that you don't appreciate all that God's done for you; it's just that when you get home from a long day at the tentmaker's, you simply have got to unwind. You need your own special oasis where you can get away from the tensions of the daily rat race. "Now," you say, "what can you do for me, Aaron?"

You watch your new leader go back to his tent, reach in and pull out the panacea for all your problems: *the groove tube.* You can be secure in knowing that by the time your children have entered high school, they will have sat under its teaching for over 22,000 hours, been indoctrinated by over 350,000 commercials, seen enough sex to make your ancestors' escape from Sodom and Gomorrah seem worthless, and enough violence to make your life-and-death struggle with the Egyptian chariots have all the excitement of a hotly contested Ping-Pong match.

So here's the scene. Moses is getting a good look at the Big Ten up on the mountain, while you and the rest of the children of Israel sit mesmerized in front of your new portable, wide-screen, living color, works-in-a-drawer orgy-maker. As the world turns, you begin to wonder if the edge of night isn't going to creep in through the dark shadows and abbreviate the days of your lives, making you all candidates for the psychiatric division of General Hospital.

And speaking of abbreviations—as you sit there desperately in need of *exercise,* you can get tired watching any number of athletes desperately in need of *rest* making millions of dollars under the aliases of NFL, AFL, WFL, NHL, WHL, NBA, ABA, and on and on and on.

Just in case you and the rest of your nomadic friends start thinking you've got your act together so well that you aren't going to be affected by all this exposure to the world, then I've got an abbreviation for you: O-S-U-R!

A young Galilean carpenter stood on an overgrown hill just off the seashore and delivered a message that makes most pulpit platitudes pale in its light. He got to the root of your problem by boldly stating,

"The eye is the lamp of the body.
   If your eye is pure,
      There will be sunshine in your soul" (*see* Luke 11:34).

But let's face it: your eyes have been seduced by a money-crazed machine, and now you are starting to believe what it tells you!

YOU'RE IN GOOD HANDS WITH AARON.

IT'S THE REAL THING—LUST IS.

YOU'VE COME A LONG WAY, BABY ISRAEL.

Now your memory of Moses is beginning to fade, and just as God is telling him:

"You must never make or worship
   Idols made of silver or gold" (*see* Exodus 20:23),

you go and melt down all of your earrings, wedding bands, and wristwatches; and maybe because of the price of beef, you bow down in a drunken stupor to your new god: a cow of gold.

Needless to say, Jehovah isn't too thrilled with your choice, and He gives Moses a piece of His Eternal Mind:

"I have seen what a stubborn, rebellious lot these people are.
   Now let me alone
      and my anger shall blaze out against them
         and destroy them all . . ." (Exodus 32:9, 10).

But Moses begs God not to do it, and the Lord changes His mind about the killing, only to add:

". . . but I will not travel among you,
   for you are a stubborn, unruly people . . ." (Exodus 33:3).

Now God has struck a chord of fear in Moses that perhaps rings louder than the fear of death itself, and one that I am most concerned with in this book. Moses replied with great anxiety:

"If you aren't going with us,
   don't let us move a step from this place.
      If you don't go with us,

who will ever know that I and my people
   have found favor with you,
   and that we are different
   from any other people
   upon the face of the earth?" (Exodus 33:15, 16).

What's the Difference?

This one ever-present factor—being "different"—was more important to Moses than anything else. His thoughts were consumed by it; it was the pulse of his existence. Nothing else seemed to matter as he risked his life many times to maintain the unique holiness of his people. The recurring theme of the first five books of the Old Testament is:

"You shall be holy,
   For I am holy."

Moses had the distinct impression that there was something unusual about the Jewish nation, and it had a lot to do with that pillar of a cloud leading them by day and the pillar of fire lighting their path by night. They were different because God traveled with them. Moses had the idea that the extraordinary victories that the Jews were winning over every foreign army they faced were a direct result of God's presence with them. As his assistant, Joshua, said:

"Today you are going to know for sure
   that the living God is among you
     and that he will, without fail,
       drive out all [your enemies]" (Joshua 3:10).

I submit to you that just as Moses expected the life of the Jew to be "different" from the life of the Gentile, expressly because the living God was with the former, so do I, as a twentieth-century follower of Jesus Christ, expect the life of the Christian to be "different" (fuller, richer, more abundant) from the life of the non-Christian. I have God's constant presence in my life, and that should make me certainly unique in a pretty predictable world. And quite frankly, I have a high regard for that individuality. Romans 12:1, 2 says that a Christian is one who gives his body over to God as a living sacrifice, and one thing I've always appreciated about living sacrifices is that just as you get ready to pigeonhole one of them and categorize its actions, it crawls right off the altar and keeps you honest.

These verses go on to state that a Christian is not a *conformist* to this world's standards, but rather he is *transformed* by his relationship with Jesus. It would be difficult for me to make you understand the sense of relief and gratitude that this truth gives me. If there is anything I *don't* want to be, it is *just like everybody else.*

Mr. Average North American is an installment buyer who spends most of his time buying things he doesn't need, with money he doesn't have, to impress people he doesn't even like. Life without Jesus is at best a circular race against time that always ends up back at the same point of frustration: no purpose and no lasting answers. I've served my stretch in that prison. No, thank you. I'd rather fill my years with life than my life with years. I'd rather not waste my days on a dead-end road. Besides, that's the easy way out, and I've always liked a challenge. Jesus said:

> "Enter by the narrow gate;
>   for the gate is wide and the way is easy,
>   that leads to destruction,
>   and those who enter by it are many.
> For the gate is narrow and the way is hard,
>   that leads to life,
>   and those who find it are few" (Matthew 7:13, 14 RSV).

We read in Proverbs 14:12 RSV: *There is a way which seems right to a man, but its end is the way of death.* This wide path that the Bible says leads to destruction may seem right; and it certainly should, since most of the world has been duped into following it. This makes it the most natural way, and—granted—it's the easiest. But it is not the *right* way.

WHEN YOUR OUTGO EXCEEDS YOUR INCOME
YOUR UPKEEP WILL BE YOUR DOWNFALL

This is not an easy day in which to raise yourself, let alone a family, and I have more than a strong hunch that this world needs the kind of flavoring that only the "salt of the earth" can give. In an article entitled "Are Americans Untrained for Sacrifice," which appeared in the *Miami Herald*, I read the following:

Many American families aren't equipped—either psychologically or with the necessary knowledge—to cope with the nation's declining economy and continued inflation. And many less-affluent families seem to be losing faith in "the American dream" of an abundant future. . . .

Many families seem unprepared or unwilling to face up to the threat of austerity and sacrifice in today's economy. Signs of stress are indicated by increased borrowing, greater reliance on credit buying, late payment of bills, and a sharp rise in personal bankruptcies.

When you put pressure on a man's pocketbook, you often strike a blow to his heart and reach him on a deep, feeling level. It would appear today that economic confusion is the name of the game. The economic atmosphere is so unstable that it seems anything could happen. There has been a new word coined in the European markets that now applies to America. It's called "stagflation." It means that our economy is stagnant while inflation is running wild.

I wouldn't have to try to alarm you, even if I wanted to, because the news media is doing a better job than I ever could. The President of the United States has declared inflation to be public enemy Number One. *Newsweek* made the gloomy picture still clearer by calling it global enemy Number One. England, West Germany, Canada, Belgium, France, Italy, and a host of other countries are at present drowning in an ocean of higher prices.

A tense feeling of unrest and insecurity seems to pervade the consumer mind-set. Many people are running scared. Not long ago, a Japanese woman jokingly started a false rumor that the prestigious Toyokawa credit bank was folding. Thirteen hours later, over 4,800 frightened depositors had withdrawn almost 5 million dollars.

Even though we can claim only 6 percent of the earth's population, the United States boasts fifteen times more goods than all the other nations combined. Still the question on everybody's lips seems to be, "How can I make ends meet?"

The University of Michigan recently published a survey which stated that over half of all American families have some kind of an installment payment or debt. I have one credit card, and I call it my mad money, because it drives me *crazy* when I have to pay off the enormous bill that it accumulates before I'm even aware that I've used it. It's an easy way to buy miracles on time or misery in installments. Charging through life makes it all too possible to find yourself forever paying for the latest fashions that just don't fit you anymore, for last year's Christmas toys that are long since broken, and expensive meals that have escaped your Epicurean memory as well as your stomach. When it comes to credit buying, you cannot afford to follow the crowd to the land of bargain-basement bankruptcy.

The way it looks from here, we are losing the Battle of Nerves with a declining world economy. The Giant of Inflation already has his hands around too many throats. Anybody for picking up five smooth stones? Just like young David, we have more ammunition than we really need to win the victory. So relax, Christian. As a "peculiar" person, your example should offer an alternative to anyone being strangled by this neurotic world with its pill-popping, uptight worriers. If I ever get an ulcer, I'm going to have a difficult time working up the necessary gall it would take to ask God to help me pay the medical bill. Tranquilizers, sleeping pills, and nervous breakdowns would do well to be excused from a Christian's life-style. God has provided for our peace of mind in the midst of tremendous anxiety and pressure.

"Peace I leave with you;
  my peace I give to you;
    not as the world gives do I give to you.
    Let not your hearts be troubled,
      neither let them be afraid" (John 14:27 RSV).

One of the most wonderful things about being a Christian is that your problems are no longer just yours. Jesus took them with Him to Calvary. Therefore:

Cast all your anxieties on him,
  for he cares about you (1 Peter 5:7 RSV).

You have five stones to work with in your anti-ulcer kit, and before they start gathering moss, you'd better get them rolling. Here they are:

1. Stop Worrying   In Luke 8:14 RSV Jesus speaks of the Word of God being "choked by the cares and riches and pleasures of life. . . ." The Greek word for "life" here is *bios* and it stands for the necessities of daily living. In other words, undue concern about the cares of life—house payments, food, utilities, clothing, cars—can choke off the effect of God's Word on your life. One of the saddest verses in the Bible comes from Paul's pen deep within the Mamertine Prison of Rome:

Do your best to visit me soon,
  for Demas has deserted me
    for love of the present world . . .
    (2 Timothy 4:9, 10 BERKELEY).

In their efforts to keep up with higher living costs, more than a few have found that the rungs on the ladder to financial success are greased with heartache and emptiness.

For the love of money is the root of all evils.
  In striving for it,
    some have wandered away from the faith
      and have pierced themselves with many sorrows
      (1 Timothy 6:10 BERKELEY).

Because God knows that money is often the index of a person's character, He spends a great deal of time dealing with money matters in the Bible. In the four Gospels, one verse in every eight deals with the proper use of material possessions, while sixteen of the thirty-eight parables deal with the same theme. Jesus is concerned with the poor trade a man is making when he "gains the whole world and loses his own soul."

In the Sermon on the Mount, He is trying to teach us how to *live*, not just how to *make a living*. I suggest that you memorize and meditate upon the crucial advice that Christ gives in Matthew 6:25–34 RSV. I love this passage. It's been invaluable to me.

"Therefore I tell you, do not be anxious about your life,
　　what you shall eat or what you shall drink,
　　　　nor about your body, what you shall put on.
　　　　　Is not life more than food,
　　　　　　and the body more than clothing?
"Look at the birds of the air:
　　they neither sow nor reap nor gather into barns,
　　　　and yet your heavenly Father feeds them.
　　　　　Are you not of more value than they?
"And which of you by being anxious
　　can add [a single moment] to his span of life?
"And why are you anxious about clothing?
　　Consider the lilies of the field, how they grow;
　　　　they neither toil nor spin;
　　　　　yet I tell you, even Solomon in all his glory
　　　　　　was not arrayed like one of these.
"But if God so clothes the grass of the field,
　　which today is alive
　　　　and tomorrow is thrown into the oven,
　　　　　will he not much more clothe you,
　　　　　　O men of little faith?
"Therefore, do not be anxious, saying,
　　'What shall we eat?' or
　　'What shall we drink?' or
　　'What shall we wear?'

For the [heathen] seek all these things;
   and your heavenly Father
     knows that you need them all.
"But seek first his kingdom and his righteousness,
   and all these things shall be yours as well.
"Therefore do not be anxious about tomorrow,
   for tomorrow will be anxious for itself.
     Let the day's own trouble
     be sufficient for the day."

That is without a doubt the greatest message that today's consumer could possibly hear. By becoming a Christian, you inherit an economic security that this world will never understand. No matter how tough the circumstances appear, the follower of Jesus stills owns a "piece of the Rock" (1 Corinthians 10:4). You can take away a Christian's trinkets, his luxuries and even his conveniences, but you can never steal his *riches*.

And my God will supply every need of yours
   according to his riches in glory in Christ Jesus
   (Philippians 4:19 RSV).

So you see, as a Christian, I am being eternally financed by the riches of Jesus. And, by the way, you can't beat the Retirement Plan either. Stop worrying, Believer. You've opened up a savings account at the First Heavenly Bank of New Jerusalem, and your stock is going up.

God's work, done in God's way, will never lack God's support.

2. Ask, and It Will Be Given You   I have already dealt in this book with the importance of a consistent, challenging prayer life. We all know that the Bible tells us to "pray without ceasing," to be "constant in prayer," to "ask and receive," and to "ask according to His will." But maybe some of you have my problem and that's why this second "stone" is so important.

I have real trouble asking anybody for anything if it's for myself. I don't know whether it's false pride or not, but it almost cost me my salvation. I've always been terrible at taking gifts, and usually feel that I have to give back twice as much as I receive. This can have a negative impact in more than one way. It has certainly kept me from having close friendships with other Christians that I really love. When I find myself in a situation where a friend is complimenting me or speaking well of my ministry, I get extremely uncomfortable and awkwardly try to change the subject. This usually cuts that person off and quenches the spirit of friendship with which he approached me. I know that part of it is my intense desire to see Jesus glorified, but a very real part is also that, as much as I need to be loved and sometimes secretly cry out for it, I'm not very good at receiving love.

You would think I would know better than that by now. I'm fully aware of how happy it makes me to give to someone else, but I tend to forget that it might richly bless a friend to do something nice for me. Luke 15:10 says that there is joy before the angels of God over one sinner who repents. The Lord and His Company enjoy giving to His children. Hebrews 12:2 states that Jesus was "willing to die a shameful death on the cross because of the joy he knew would be his afterwards. . . ."

Please join me in practicing the art of "asking and receiving." For starters, the Bible says:

For the wages of sin is death,
    but the free gift of God is eternal life
        in Christ Jesus our Lord (Romans 6:23 RSV).

Out of the ten major religions, only one is "peculiar" enough to be based on *grace*. All of the others are contrived religions of rules and regulations in which the believer must work hard all of his life for a chance at some nebulous state of bliss. In Christianity, God so loved the world that He came all the way down, passed the point of no return, and met man on the common ground of the death and Resurrection of His only Son, Jesus. Ask Christ into your life, and you will *receive* the gift from that moment on.

3. Seek, and You Will Find   What I especially like about this "stone" is that you know it best by throwing it and not by inspecting it. Surely this is the one that David used to make an impression on Goliath.

Faith is an action word. It always has been. Even though salvation is a free gift, I don't believe it implies that the recipient must passively sit back and take it all in. May I remind you that we have been invited to share in the fellowship of His sufferings. I'm glad that Jesus never said, "If you obey me, then I will love you." No, that would be salvation by works. Instead He stated, "If you love me, then you will obey me" (*see* John 14:15). That's *salvation by grace*, but I emphasize here the word *obey*.

Jesus became the Author of eternal salvation
For all who obey Him (*see* Hebrews 5:9 AMPLIFIED).

And He declares:

"If you adhere to My teaching,
you will truly be My disciples" (John 8:31 BERKELEY).

My point is simply this: Christianity is not freeloading on Jesus. Inspiration is well followed by perspiration.

To seek is

To sweat,
To work,
To obey,
To love,
To do,
To learn,
To find.

4. Knock, and It Will Be Opened to You   It has always been interesting to me that, translated literally, Matthew 7:7 actually says, "Keep on knocking, and the door will be opened to you." This implies a persistent, almost bulldoglike quality that it would be good for more Christians to emulate in these critical times.

Daniel never stopped knocking even when the situation looked hopeless. As a result, a lion's den turned into a menagerie for kitty-cats. I remember the insight I received when I first read about Jacob's wrestling match with the Lord at Peniel (Genesis

32:24–32). Jacob simply would not let go, even though he was suffering, until the Lord gave him a blessing. Cream eventually comes to the top, even if it takes some of us a little longer than others. Just keep on knocking.

Some of you are planning a nervous breakdown. You've worked hard for it. You deserve it. But before you get it, I encourage you to trade in your life on the razor's edge of tension and anxiety for the door that opens up into the green pastures of salvation (John 10:9). Just keep on knocking.

When you open the door to God's House and walk in by faith, please notice that it is filled with people. You cannot be a Christian and be an island at the same time. There is no such animal as an isolated believer. Jesus said:

"So whatever you wish that men would do to you,
     do so to them;
          for this is the law and the prophets" (Matthew 7:12 RSV).

5. Build on the Rock   It doesn't matter how strong your legs are if you take your stand upon quicksand. This is precisely why it is so important for you to base your life on something solid, something eternal: like a Rock:

And no one can ever lay any other real foundation
     than the one we already have—
          Jesus Christ (1 Corinthians 3:11).

". . . I am sending Christ to be the carefully chosen,
     precious Cornerstone of my church . . ." (1 Peter 2:6).

Don't put your trust in earthly treasures. We've already seen how quickly they rot away. If you build your life with the "wood, hay, and stubble" that this decaying world system offers, then you must be ready for it all to be burned up on the final day of Judgment (*see* 1 Corinthians 3:13–15). Jesus said it like this:

"Every one then who hears these words of mine
     and does them will be like a wise man
          who built his house upon the rock;

and the rain fell, and the floods came,
   and the winds blew and beat upon that house,
      but it did not fall,
         Because it had been founded on the rock"
         (Matthew 7:24, 25 RSV).

The alternative to building on the Rock is eventually to see your life destroyed by the rains of corruption, the floods of sin, and the winds of evil.

When you have little children, you also have the privilege of reacquainting yourself with that wonderful nightly ritual called the bedtime story. When I come home from a road trip, I step right back into the role of Ye Olde Storyteller. My son and I have a favorite fable; you probably know it as "The Three Little Pigs," only we've changed it a little. Christopher is the piglet who builds his house out of straw; my wife is the sow in charge of the house of sticks; and—because I tell the story—I'm the preacher-pig who wisely builds a church of brick. The story really gets exciting when Jesus makes a surprise appearance at the end of the story and beats up the wolf! Walt Disney never had it so good.

Perhaps this is why I like this final parable in the Sermon on the Mount so much. It makes sense to me. I can relate to it. I've built my house upon the Rock and I like the results.

As you finish this book, I encourage you not to stop with the reaction given by those who first heard His Sermon. The Bible says:

And when Jesus finished these sayings,
   the crowds were astonished at his teaching,
      for he taught them as one who had authority,
         and not as their scribes (Matthew 7:28, 29 RSV).

Don't stop with mere amazement at the unusual honesty and awesome compassion of this Jesus of Nazareth. His message is meant for you personally.

"Come to me,
   all who labor and are heavy laden,
      and I will give you rest" (Matthew 11:28 RSV).

I haven't written this book for financial profit or just to keep myself off the streets at night. I had you in mind the whole time. If you are a Christian, then act like one. Be different. Be *peculiar*, transformed from this world's standards. Christianity is not compromise, it's conversion.

Christianity is
      "Christ-in-you-ity"
         "Christ-in-me-ity"

Christ *for* us is encouraging; Christ *with* us is a beautiful thought; but Christ *in* us is our only hope of glory (Colossians 1:27).

You will get tired of straining and complaining. Try the joy that comes in just "containing"!

7
Good News for You

So you want to be different? You think you need a few changes in your life? I challenge you to read through the following five principles which I've listed below. Take the time—and become a part of *A World of Differents.*

> The Bible teaches that God loves you.
> He loves you so much that He gave to
> the world its greatest gift. . . .
> THE GIFT OF HIS SON.

> God has provided us with a plan
> that, if followed, has as its reward—
> Eternal Life . . . STARTING TODAY.

> 1 Timothy 2:4–6 says it this way:

. . . he [God] longs for all to be saved and to understand this truth: that God is on one side and all the people on the other side, and Christ Jesus, himself man, is between them to bring them together, by living his life for all mankind.

THAT'S GOOD NEWS!

1. GOD LOVES YOU

. . . he [God] longs for all to be saved. . . .
                                1 Timothy 2:4

For God loved the world so much that he gave **his only Son** so that anyone who believes in him shall not perish but have eternal life.

                                        John 3:16

But God showed his great love for us by sending **Christ** to die for us while we were still sinners.

                                        Romans 5:8

2. SIN IS SEPARATION

. . . God is on one side and all the people on the other side. . . .
                                1 Timothy 2:5

Since the beginning of time man has willfully gone his own way . . . disobeying God. This disobedience causes **spiritual separation** with God.

Yes, all have sinned; all fall short of God's glorious ideal.
                                Romans 3:23

For the wages of sin is death, but the free gift of God is **eternal life** through Jesus Christ our Lord.

                                        Romans 6:23

3. JESUS IS THE BRIDGE

... Christ Jesus, himself man, is between them to bring them together, by giving his life for all mankind.

1 Timothy 2:5, 6

[Jesus said ...] "I am the way—yes, and the Truth and the Life. No one can get to the Father except by means of me."

John 14:6

For if you tell others with your own mouth that Jesus Christ is your Lord, and believe in your own heart that God has raised him from the dead, you will be saved.

Romans 10:9

**So it is up to you. . . . The choice is yours.
If you want to follow Jesus, pray a prayer
like this and He will come into your life.**

*Lord Jesus, please come into my life and be
my Saviour and Lord. Make me the person You
want me to be. Thank You for giving me the gift
of eternal life and for forgiving my sins. Amen.*

4. GOD'S *FOREVER FAMILY*

If you sincerely prayed, Christ is in your life. You may not feel anything, but feelings are not to be trusted. Claim the **fact** of your new life.

Welcome to God's FOREVER FAMILY!

My Decision for Christ

Today I start a new and *different* adventure. I've decided to change directions in my life . . . to really put the past behind me and keep Jesus in front of me. With the help of the Holy Spirit, study of God's Word, prayer, and fellowship with other Christians, I'm looking forward to doing my part to help change the world.

Signed_____

Date_____

5. PASS IT ON

Share this new life with others. God wants to use you! God's best to you as you help others discover *A World of Differents*.